BLACK RIVER
IN THE
NORTH COUNTRY

BLACK RIVER

IN THE

NORTH COUNTRY

HOWARD THOMAS

1985

NORTH COUNTRY BOOKS, INC.

18 Irving Place
UTICA, NEW YORK 13501

FIRST PRINTING 1963

SECOND PRINTING 1974

THIRD PRINTING 1978

FOURTH PRINTING 1985

ISBN 978-1-4930-7677-2

FOREWORD

Thomas C. O'Donnell launched a trilogy on the Black River with *Birth of a River* in 1952 and completed the second volume, *The River Rolls on*, in 1959. He died in 1962, leaving the project unfinished. As his friend, I felt that I should undertake the third book, and the result is *Black River in the North Country*.

In my study of the Black River, I discovered that any story of progress along that stream and its tributaries has been colored by industry and water-power development, so emphasis in this book has been placed on those phases of river life, to the consequent neglect of politics, religion, etc. A function of the third book of a trilogy is to recapitulate material embodied in all three books and to bring the story up to date. I have not only described lumbering, boating, paper-making, heavy industry and hydro-electric development along the Black River and its tributaries, but have endeavored to discuss present conditions in the chapter entitled, "A River Ramble."

No two writers assemble material in the same way or write about it in an identical manner. Mr. O'Donnell had a flair for the homey anecdote and the ability to glean choice nuggets of information from old-timers. Much of the material in this book has been gained from reading, and my conversations with people have been made in an effort to elicit facts about the Black River valley.

The task has not been easy. The last history of Lewis County was published in 1883 and, with the exception of Harry F. Landon's *North Country*, no comprehensive volume on Jefferson County has appeared for 60 years. Bringing the story of the Black River down to the present time has involved explorations of newspaper files, the use of available city and village histories, and many conversations with people who are familiar with the history of the area.

The most rewarding phase of this research has resulted from my contacts with citizens of the North Country. Everyone I approached was friendly and anxious to be of assistance. Villagers took time to sit down with me and point out phases of life in their communities. Industrialists halted their business activities to help me with the histories of their organizations and to shower me with pamphlets containing vital information. Space does not permit listing the names of all these individuals, but I wish to express my appreciation to each and every one who lent me a hand.

For reading and research privileges extended to me, I wish to thank the Jefferson County Historical Society and the *Watertown Daily Times*. Two individuals deserve special words of appreciation: Dr. John M. Gaus of Prospect not only put his valuable library at my disposal but lent advice on the manuscript; David F. Lane of Watertown straightened me out on several knotty points of history and kindly read the first half of the manuscript.

It is my hope that *Black River in the North Country* will provide information and enjoyment to readers in the Black River valley and elsewhere.

June, 1963   HOWARD THOMAS

CONTENTS

ILLUSTRATIONS

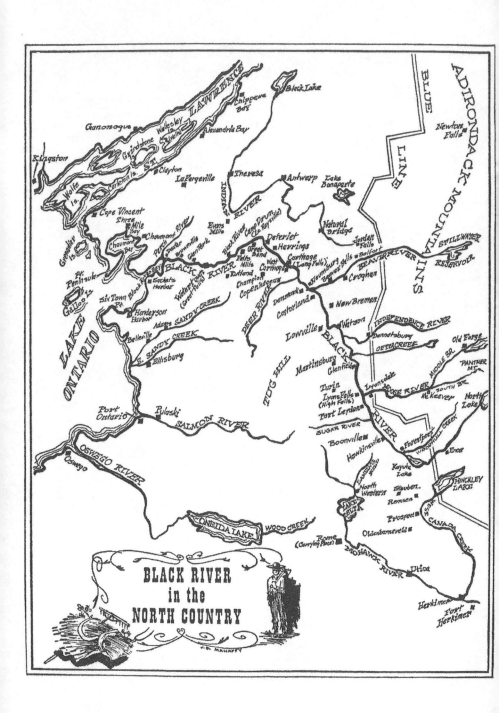

BLACK RIVER
in the
NORTH COUNTRY

J. D. MAHAFFY

I
BLACK RIVER IN THE
NORTH COUNTRY

NATURE PLAYED A SLY JOKE on the Black River in the North
Country. Instead of permitting it to flow generally from west
to east, like the St. Lawrence and the Mohawk, she established its source high in the Adirondack wilderness and
mapped its course northward to the great bend and westward
to Lake Ontario, in that way making it a geographical freak
which was totally ignored during the early settlement of
North America. French colonization followed the St. Lawrence in a southwesterly direction. English expansion moved
westward through the Mohawk valley. The apex of these
two drives to conquer a continent was Choueguen (Oswego)
on Lake Ontario, where the conflicting forces met. To the
east, a life-and-death struggle was going on for possession of
the Hudson River–Lake Champlain area. The Black River,
draining nearly 2,000 square miles in the North Country and
lying in the triangle formed by the Adirondacks on the east,
the Mohawk River, Oneida Lake and the Oswego River on
the south and west, and the St. Lawrence River and Lake Ontario on the north, might have been Patagonia as far as the
struggle for control of North America was concerned. In
short, the trend of exploration and settlement was along east-
west lines. The Black River simply flowed in the wrong direction. No map earlier than 1800 traced the course of the Black
River accurately; to map-makers prior to that year, the North
Country was merely the beaver-hunting grounds of the
Oneida and Onondaga Indians.

These Indians did not hold the North Country in high regard, though their trails crossed it in many places and evi-

dences of Indian forts could be traced by the first white settlers. Nature also played a hand in this spurning of the Black River region, for she bestowed upon it a severity of climate which none but the most rugged human beings could endure. The Indians did not choose to be that rugged; when the temperatures dropped below zero, and the North Country was transformed into a vast island of swirling snow, they retreated to the comparative comfort of the St. Lawrence and Mohawk river valleys.

The wars between the Iroquois and their Canadian enemies, the long struggle between the French and British, and the shorter war for American independence, were all fought along east-west lines involving the St. Lawrence and the Mohawk rivers and, at the confluence of the two routes, Lake Ontario at Choueguen. Mention of the Black River country during these wars consisted of reports of raiding parties or scouting expeditions which cut through the North Country to reach objectives on the Mohawk or the St. Lawrence, or retreated along Indian trails to Lake Ontario or to Fort Stanwix, now Rome.

During these centuries of warfare, the longest river lying completely within the borders of the State of New York was pouring its coffee-colored water into Lake Ontario after flowing about 115 miles through the North Country from its source in what is now Herkimer County. In the upper part of its course, from North Lake to the High Falls (Lyons Falls), the Black River is a surging, tumbling stream, falling 320 feet between Forestport and the High Falls, where it is joined by the Moose, a truly rambunctious river with branches rising in and near the Fulton Chain of lakes. At the High Falls, the combined streams cascade 60 feet and seem obsessed with the idea of hurtling their way to Lake Ontario. Instead, the Black River from the High Falls to the Long Falls (Carthage) settles into a placid stream which drops but ten feet in over forty miles. Four main tributaries, the Deer River from the west, and the Otter, Independence and Beaver from the east, empty their water into the Black between the High Falls and the Long Falls without disturbing its placid course except in spring, when the added flow of their water, plus the contribution of the Moose, cause the Black to overflow its banks and create what is known locally as "Lake Lewis." At the Long Falls, the Black River reverts to its original character; over the 31 miles to Lake Ontario, it tumbles for the most part in a frenzied manner about 480 feet, the most important descent being at the Great Falls (Watertown), where it drops over 100 feet.

This peculiar personality has bestowed both prosperity and ruin on the North Country. Water power on the Black River and its tributaries has turned the wheels of industry for over 160 years. The long, calm stretch provided navigation facilities for the Black River Canal. On the debit side, the river at certain seasons of the year exhibits a lack of control preeminent among rivers of the State. Disastrous floods have caused heavy property damage over the years, both through destruction of dams, mills and bridges, and by the annual flooding of the land between Lowville and Carthage, with resultant injury to arable soil. Low water in mid-summer seriously handicaps industries dependent upon the stream for power. This precarious behavior of the Black River has led to much agitation for better control, the latest being in 1955, when the proposal to build a control dam on the Moose near Panther Mountain was defeated in a referendum by the voters of the State.

Despite these headaches, the Black River has aided the North Country. Its only city, Watertown, owes its growth mainly to the multifarious industries which have flourished on Beebee's Island and Sewall's Island. For over fifty years, the river was used for navigation between the High Falls and the Long Falls, thus aiding the lumbering and dairying industries of Lewis County. Water power provided by the river and its tributaries has encouraged paper-making at Lyons Falls, Beaver Falls, Carthage, Deferiet, Watertown, Brownville and

Dexter. And, more recently, Black River water has furnished hydro-electric power to turn the wheels of industry and to provide electric lighting for the whole North Country.

This split personality is not confined to the river, but extends to the soil on either side of the stream. The eastern hinterland, stretching back to the Adirondacks and extending down the river from its source to beyond the Long Falls, is not suited to agriculture, for its basic rock, gneiss, has but a thin covering of arable soil. Attempts to develop its ore deposits have been made over the years, but the chief resource of this eastern sector is timber, and the great logging operations of the latter part of the nineteenth century extended up the tributaries and into the Adirondack forest. The soil to the west of the river, however, is basically either Trenton limestone or Black River limestone, and a vast arable area extends from above Lowville down through Rutland, Champion and Adams and across the great bend in the river to Lake Ontario. This section has been the granary and dairy of the North Country since the days of the first settlers.

North Country climate has always received a bad press. Way back in 1807, a snow storm set in on the 31st of March and continued until the 5th of April. Snow lay five feet deep on the level. There followed the first of the great floods which have harassed the Black River valley. The river, swollen by rapidly melting snow, raced through its channel at breakneck speed, taking away dams, mills and bridges all along its course.

Winters are long in the North Country. In 1813, Denmark got two feet of snow on October 12th, and the same town, in 1824, had a four-inch snowfall on May 14th. Two years later, also on May 14th, a three-foot fall of snow in Denmark broke down fruit trees which were in full bloom. On April 17, 1835, Dyer Huntington of Watertown complained to his diary: "Am of the opinion that the Black River country was created for such inhabitants only as woodchucks, hedgehogs and skunks!" Not so many years ago, an old-timer remarked:

"We have nine months of winter and four months of damned poor weather. It's no wonder the Indians got out and left it to us."

North Country climate is really not as bad as it has been pictured. True, winters are severe, with temperatures running down to 35 or so below zero, and the ground covered with a blanket of snow from the Adirondack foothills to Lake Ontario. Outsiders, though generally solicitous, sometimes like to poke fun at the Black River region and call it the "snow-belt of the United States."

Critics of North Country climate choose to forget the glorious days of late spring, when the Black River valley blossoms forth in sheer joy at the passing of winter, and trout rise to flies on the upper stretches of the river. They overlook the summer days so endearing to vacationists around Black River Bay, where sailboats spread their white wings against cloudless skies; and the cool nights which bring refreshing sleep to jaded city-dwellers. Autumn in the North Country can be rarely beautiful, with splashes of color from the deciduous trees flaming against the deep green of Adirondack pine, spruce and hemlock.

The North Country has a cleanliness about it. Smog and air pollution are absent. Crisp breezes off Lake Ontario may make trees around Copenhagen lean as they grow, but they put roses in the cheeks of North Country girls. Over the years since the first New Englanders fought their way through the wilderness, inhabitants of the North Country have become reconciled to the capriciousness of the Black River and to the rigors of winters which make them probably the healthiest people in the State.

The winter of 1962–1963 was probably the most severe within the memory of the oldest settler, but the North Country took it in stride, though it was the recipient of a bad press from the Atlantic to the Pacific. The voice of the North Country, the *Watertown Daily Times*, replied editorially: "As much as we respect the good wishes and concern of friends all over the country for our welfare during the recent several days of heavy snows and winds, it is only proper to point out that they have become exercised from exaggerated accounts of what happened. Most of us are quite snug, comfortable and adequately housed and more than adequately fed. To be sure, the snow has been deep, roads difficult, and a few were blocked. There was the normal number of emergency type situation, collapsed roofs and difficult dislocations. Winters are always like that, but some are more so . . . We regret that our friends and relatives in distant points have worried needlessly about us. We are sorry we can't do anything about the reason for their worries. They just got the wrong information. Our obituaries were premature. For proof, these friends and well-wishers should have been here during the past week. In fact, we invite them to come now and enjoy themselves. The weather is exhilarating; the snow is deep and the snow banks are high, the kind of attraction that many people would enjoy."

II
THE PATH OF EMPIRE

THE EARLY HISTORY of the Black River in the North Country might be termed "iffy," for a scarcity of written records and the inaccuracy of maps have led to much conjecture on the part of historians.

The North Country was inhabited long before the beginnings of written history, for it was lined with Indian trails and studded with Indian fortifications. Dr. Franklin B. Hough, in his *History of Jefferson County*, mentioned traces of fortifications which he had visited, or about which he had learned, in Brownville, Hounsfield, Le Ray, Rutland, Watertown and other towns. These rude forts, ostensibly for defense against attack, were usually constructed along the banks of streams and were irregularly semi-circular, the open side facing the stream, the wings of the embankments extending down the slope and curving inward to prevent flanking movements by an enemy. Early settlers found, in or near these forts, fragments of hearths, bits of rude pottery, stone chisels and bones of animals and of human beings.

Dr. Hough described one of these fortifications, located in the town of Rutland: "It is on the summit of the Trenton limestone terrace, which forms a bold escarpment, extending down the river, and passing across the southern part of Watertown. There here occurs a slight embankment, and ditch irregularly oval, with several gateways; and along the ditch, in several places, have been found great numbers of skeletons, almost entirely of males, and lying in great confusion, as if they had been slain in defending it. Among these bones were those of a man of colossal size, *and like nine-tenths of the others, furnished with a row of double teeth in each jaw.* This singular peculiarity, with that of broad flat jaws, retreating forehead, and great prominence in the occiput, which was common to most of the skulls, may hereafter afford some clue to their history. There is said to have been found at this place by excavating, hearths, or fire places, with bones of animals, broken pottery, and implements of stone, *at two different levels,* separated by an accumulation of earth and vegetable mould from one to two feet thick, as if the place had been twice occupied. So great has been the length of time since these bones have been covered, that they fall to pieces very soon after being exposed to the air. Charred corn, bones, and relics, occur at both levels, but more abundantly at the lower. At numerous places, not exhibiting traces of fortification, are found fire places, accumulations of chips, of flint, and broken pottery; as if these points had been occupied as dwellings. In several places, *bone pits* have been found, where human remains in great numbers have been accumulated."

These primitive Indians may have owned kinship to the mound builders of western New York and Ohio, but they were in a less advanced stage. Who were they? Rev. W. M. Beauchamp, an authority on Indians, said in a talk before the Jefferson County Historical Society in 1886: "I answer without hesitation, that in the main, though not entirely, they were members of the Huron Iroquois family."

These fort-builders seldom settled for any length of time in one place, but used the Black River wilderness as a hunting ground and as a battle ground for years of intermittent warfare which resulted in a clean-cut victory for the Iroquois. The North Country became the acknowledged hunting ground of the Oneidas and the Onondagas. Tug Hill was the "happy hunting ground," because deer would flounder in the heavy snow and Indians could overtake and slaughter them.

The Iroquois were in control of the North Country when Samuel de Champlain became the first Governor of New France in 1603. The two chiefs he killed with his arquebus in the Lake Champlain country were Mohawks; by this act, Champlain alienated the Iroquois and brought about the downfall of the French empire in North America 160 years later.

Champlain may have been the first white man of importance to set eyes on the mouth of the Black River, though he made no mention of that stream in a report of his expedition of 1615, which culminated in his humiliating defeat at Nichols Pond in Madison County. Champlain was searching for the Northwest Passage when he paddled up the St. Lawrence and Ottawa rivers that summer. After discovering Lake Huron, he returned through what is now the province of Ontario and reached Lake Ontario near the Bay of Quinte.

Here is what he wrote: "We continued along the border of Entouhonorous (Lake Ontario) always hunting . . . being there we crossed over at one of the extremities, extending eastward, which is the beginning of the River St. Lawrence, in the parallel of forty three degrees of latitude. There are some beautiful and very large islands in this passage. We made about fourteen leagues to cross to the other side of the lake, proceeding southward toward the enemy's country. The Indians concealed all their canoes in the woods near the bank. We traveled by land about four leagues over a sandy plain, where I observed a very pleasing and fine country, watered by numerous small streams, and two little rivers which empty into said lake, and a number of ponds and prairies, where there was an infinite quantity of game, a great many vines and fine trees, vast numbers of chestnuts, the fruit of which was yet to shell. It is quite small but well flavored."

Champlain's account is open to all kinds of conjecture. He travelled fourteen leagues by water; inasmuch as the ancient league varied from two to over four miles, his trip must have covered between 28 and about 60 miles. Did he take the Canadian channel around Wolfe Island and the American channel to Cape Vincent? Were the "very large islands" Wolfe and Grenadier? Harry F. Landon in *North Country* wrote that, inasmuch as four leagues was about the distance from Henderson Harbor to Salmon River, Champlain hid his canoes at the former place and marched to the latter. The two little rivers add to the confusion. Were they the two branches of Sandy Creek? And, more important, did Champlain see the mouth of the Black River? It seems rather unlikely.

The followers of St. Ignatius Loyola, a missionary group of French priests known as Jesuits or Black Robes, arrived in New France early in the seventeenth century. The Jesuits made an unfavorable impression on the Mohawks, who tortured and killed Father Isaac Jogues and his companions; but their man-to-man treatment of Indians impressed the Onondagas.

These Jesuits may have been the first white men to see the Black River, both at the mouth and in the interior, though there is a possibility that the *courier de bois*, the French fur traders, antedated them. Inasmuch as these men of the woods

kept no written records, the first account of travel in the
Black River country came from the pen of Father Antoine
Poncet, who passed through the area in 1653 under unfavorable circumstances, for the Indians had lopped off two of his
fingers and were escorting him as a prisoner. Most historians
think he came over from the Onondaga country toward what
is now Ogdensburg, but Nellis B. Crouse, a Utica historian,
thought that the Indians left the Mohawk Valley and came
up the West Canada Creek and plunged into the wilderness
to Cranberry Lake and down the Oswegatchie River.

Father Simon Le Moyne, in 1654, made his first visit to
the Onondagas. He came up the St. Lawrence from Montreal
with a single companion. They landed at Chippewa Bay and
again near Clayton, at which point they followed French
Creek and the Chaumont River to Chaumont Bay. They por-
taged over Point Peninsula with the aid of some Hurons, who
gave them food. Did they follow the outline of Black River
Bay? They did not say.

On his return, Le Moyne paddled along the shore of Lake
Ontario until he reached what he described as an ideal place
for a settlement. He wrote: "There are beautiful prairies here
and good fishing." Landon wrote: "It is thought that this
place was somewhere within the Black River Bay or Henderson Harbor because Le Moyne speaks of islands, on one of
which he took refuge when his canoe overturned."

The Jesuits made many trips to the Onondagas. Their usual
stopping place was at the mouth of the Salmon River. One
Jesuit description of this place has attracted the attention of
all historians: "In the spring as soon as the snows melt it is
full of gold-colored fish; next come carp, and finally achigen.
The latter is a flat fish half a foot long and of very fine flavor.
Then comes the brill and at the end of May, when straw-
berries are ripe, sturgeon are killed with hatchets. All the rest
of the year until winter the salmon furnishes food to the village Onontae. We made our bed last night on the shore of a

lake where natives toward the end of winter, break the ice and catch fish—or rather draw them up by the bucketfuls."

In June, 1672, Louis de Bouade, Comte de Frontenac, Governor of New France, held a great powwow with the three western nations of the Iroquois at Cataracqui, near the present site of Kingston, Ontario. Fort Frontenac, built at Cataracqui, became the chief outpost of the French until it was taken by Col. John Bradstreet and the British in 1758.

Frontenac's successor, M. Le Febvre de la Barre, left Fort Frontenac on August 21, 1684 with an army of 1,800 French regulars, Canadians and Indians and landed at the mouth of the Salmon River for a powwow with the Indians. The low ground and a scarcity of fish—the salmon were no longer there—caused a large number of de la Barre's men to sicken and die. This expedition started the controversy over the location of La Famine or Hungry Bay. Two surveyors around 1800 thought that the name applied to Black River Bay. Charles C. Brodhead so noted it on his map but spelled it "Hungary Bay." Benjamin Wright said Henderson Harbor was located "along Hungry Bay." Arthur Pound, author of *Lake Ontario*, placed Hungry Bay at the mouth of the Salmon River, where de la Barre's men sickened and died.

Legends say that the Indians who attacked Fort Frontenac and murdered and scalped French settlers at La Chine near Montreal in 1679 stopped at an island near the point where the St. Lawrence River leaves Lake Ontario. The wilder rumors have the Indians making a meal out of the bones and hearts of Frenchmen.

Frontenac, in 1696, during his second term as Governor, camped with his army at Isle aux Chevreuls while en route to an unsuccessful expedition against the Onondagas. This island was known to the British as Deer or Buck Island and later as Carleton Island.

At the outbreak of the French and Indian War, the rulers of New France had designs against British forts Bull, Newport and Williams, which guarded the Carrying Place from the Mohawk River to Wood Creek on the route to Oswego. On March 17th, 1756, M. Gaspard de Chassemy de Lery, with a force of French regulars, Canadians and Indians (Iroquois, Algonquins and Nipissings), left Montreal, skated up the St. Lawrence to La Presentation (Ogdensburg) and took Indian trails to the Mohawk Valley.

De Lery's route after leaving La Presentation has led to disagreements among historians. Most of them say merely that he came down through the Black River country. Landon thought he took the Oswegatchie trail, which went up the Oswegatchie River to Black Lake, and by a portage to the Indian River, then up that river and across to the Black River, and on to the Mohawk River or West Canada Creek. Tharratt Gilbert Best, in *North Country Life, Spring, 1960,* said De Lery followed the Black River as far as present Boonville, then took the Lansingkill and Mohawk River valleys to the Carrying Place. Crouse was of the same opinion. A dissenting voice came from Rev. Beauchamp, who said: "M. de Lery, with 300 men, came from La Presentation to Salmon River—not Black —and followed the route of the Rome and Watertown railroad from Pulaski to Fort Bull."

Regardless which trail De Lery took, he arrived at Fort Bull early in the morning of March 27th, after ten days in the wilderness. The fort fell an easy victim to the surprise attack. The garrison was massacred; the fort and its supplies were destroyed. De Lery, having accomplished his mission, took his men into the woods to pray, and retreated toward La Presentation. En route, he stopped at Riviere de la Famine. Black or Salmon?

The route which M. de Belletre took in his Mohawk Valley raid in 1757 is also open to dispute. Crouse and other historians said he used trails through the Black River country known only to Indians. Rev. Beauchamp insisted that he went from the Salmon River to the Carrying Place, where the men crossed the Mohawk, either by swimming or by wading in water up to their necks, and marched down the northern side of the river to the Palatine settlement at Herkimer, which they destroyed.

Henderson Harbor got involved in Marquis de Montcalm's expedition to take Oswego in 1756. Montcalm sent ahead Sieur Colon de Villiers to build, at the tip of Six-Town Point, a crude fort or observation post to protect the portage at the head of Stony Creek. Montcalm's army camped at Henderson Harbor.

The Black River country saw no more Frenchmen for the rest of the war, but Grenadier Island became the point of rendezvous for the forces of Geoffrey Lord Amherst which captured Montreal in 1760 and practically put an end to the war, though the treaty of peace was signed three years later.

Deer or Buck Island became a gathering place for British forces during the American Revolution. Shortly before the outbreak of hostilities, merchants from Quebec had built several stores on the island to further their profitable trade with the Six Nations and the Western Indians. In 1775, the British government established a supply base there, and quartermaster stores were shipped from Quebec and Montreal.

Sir John Johnson and his Tories, forced to leave Johnstown in 1776, wound their way through the wilderness via Arietta and Raquette Lake, where they left their snowshoes, an act which may have bestowed a name on that body of water. They gathered on Deer Island and formed the Royal Greens, with Col. John Butler in command.

Col. Barry St. Leger left Montreal with a force of regulars, Greens and Indians in late June, 1777. Inasmuch as his objective was Fort Stanwix (Rome), he ordered Col. Daniel Claus to send John O'Hare, Chief John Odiseruney and a party of Indians to reconnoitre the fort. John Alden Scott, the authority on the siege of Fort Stanwix, thought this party came down the Black River, Lansingkill and Mohawk River valleys. St. Leger's army camped for ten days on Deer Island before sailing down the southern shore of Lake Ontario to Oswego, from which point it advanced up the Oswego River, Oneida

Lake and Wood Creek to besiege Fort Stanwix. After St. Leger's failure to take this strategic point at the Carrying Place, the regulars and the Greens retreated to Oswego.

This retreat played a part in the confusion over the location of Hungry Bay. John A. Haddock, in his *History of Jefferson County*, contended that St. Leger sailed for Montreal, leaving his soldiers to get back any way they could. The soldiers embarked, chiefly in batteaux, and ran into a terrific storm off Point Peninsula. Several batteaux were driven across the Point into Chaumont Bay. Many soldiers were drowned, the boats were wrecked, and most of the provisions were lost. The survivors wandered about in the woods, bewildered and starving. Hence, Hungry Bay. A party of Indians gave the men food, helped them to bury their military chests, and piloted them to Deer Island.

Sir Frederick Haldimand, who succeeded Sir Guy Carleton as Governor General of Canada, decided to fortify Deer Island, which he renamed Carleton Island after his predecessor. The construction of Fort Haldimand, which guarded the eastern channel of the St. Lawrence River, went on for the remainder of the war. The fort stood at the edge of a cliff, was built chiefly of stone, and was protected in the rear by an earthwork, a ditch and an outer parapet of stone.

Haddock maintained that the caves at Cape Vincent served as hiding places for scouts sent out from Fort Stanwix to watch the building of Fort Haldimand, and that letters from these scouts mentioned a cave "where they rested in security and by going only a few steps from which they had a complete view of the island."

Scouts and raiders evidently penetrated the Black River country. In 1779, Lieuts. Hardenburgh and McClellan were sent out from Fort Stanwix, ostensibly to take La Presentation by surprise, but really to distract the Oneidas from Col. Goose Van Schaick's expedition against the Onondagas. This party probably came along the Oswegatchie Trail and returned by the same route. It engaged in a brief skirmish with the British before La Presentation, realized that the fort could not be taken, and retreated to Fort Stanwix. In the meantime, Van Schaick had destroyed the Onondaga villages.

Fort Haldimand housed some of the Greens and other Tories during the winter of 1779–1780. Among them was Molly Brant, common law wife of Sir William Johnson and sister of the great Thayendanegea. Capt. Fraser, in command at the fort, had a hard time keeping "Miss Molly" in "good temper," as was recommended by Gov. Haldimand. Molly wanted a house built, and had her way, for Fraser wrote to Haldimand that she had "got into her new house and seems better satisfied than I have ever seen her."

Tories and Indians may have stopped at Lowville, probably after Sir John Johnson's great raid of the Mohawk Valley in the autumn of 1780. A Lowville legend persists that a war party camped near the village and that it was returning from a raid on the Mohawk Valley. The Tories and Indians had paddled down the Black River from the High Falls in canoes they had hidden there. They spent a night on a flat rock near Lowville, where they had a cache of corn. The next day, they went on toward Carleton Island.

With this party was a woman captive who was pregnant. She gave birth to a daughter while at Carleton Island. This girl returned to the Black River country after the war, married a veteran of the Battle of Oriskany, and lived to be 100 years old.

The last raid from Carleton Island was that of Maj. John Ross and Capt. Walter Butler in the autumn of 1781. Haldimand's plan involved a union at Oswego of Ross' forces from Carleton Island and Butler's Rangers from Fort Niagara. The combined forces left Oswego on October 10th, hid their boats at Oneida Lake, and made a swift march south of the Mohawk River. Scouts from Fort Plain discovered them at Sharon Springs. When the raiders attacked settlers near Fort Hunter, where the Schoharie Creek enters the Mohawk River, Col. Marinus Willett, commandant at Fort Plain, gathered his forces and set out after them.

Ross knew that he had lost the element of surprise, and that he could not return to his boats at Oneida Lake. He made a show of resistance at Johnstown and headed across country in an attempt to find the Oswegatchie Trail.

Willett caught up with him at a fording place on the West Canada Creek, probably in the present town of Ohio. Butler was killed and scalped. Ross headed for Carleton Island. Willett put it tersely: "In this situation to the compassion of a Starving Wilderness we left them."

Seven days later, Ross, minus the Indians and some Raiders who chose to return to Fort Niagara, arrived on Carleton Island, having lost but ten other men in the retreat from Johnstown. He was forced to cross several streams swollen by rain and melting snow, and had to construct rude rafts to get his men across. One or possibly more of these "several" streams was the Black River, which changes its course at the great bend.

Ross continued in command of Fort Haldimand until he was sent to take charge of Fort Ontario at Oswego. He was the British officer who received the news of the treaty of peace in 1783, brought up by messengers sent from the Mohawk Valley by Col. Willett.

The British kept possession of Fort Haldimand and the forts at Oswego and Niagara long after the treaty had been signed. The fort on Carleton Island, manned by a small force of invalid soldiers, deteriorated during these years. Surveyors in 1796 found a corporal and three men in charge. Most of the guns had been taken to Fort York (Toronto).

In 1808, when the United States wanted to station troops on Carleton Island, Maj. F. McKenzie at Kingston replied that his orders were to retain Carleton Island, and that he would implicitly observe them.

III
OPENING THE WILDERNESS

THE VICTORIOUS American war for independence extended the boundaries of the new nation to Lake Ontario and the St. Lawrence River. And, at the Treaty of Fort Stanwix, signed on September 22, 1788, the Iroquois relinquished their hunting grounds in the North Country, with the exception of a small plot reserved by the Oneidas. Northern New York was thrown open for sale by commissioners appointed by Governor George Clinton for that purpose.

These commissioners were in control of the least-known tract of land in the State, the vast area stretching from the Adirondack foothills to Lake Ontario. They could rely merely on reports brought in by scouts who had traversed it during the late war, and the inaccurate descriptions of the Indians.

Existing maps were of little assistance. Champlain drew a crude map from memory way back in 1632, on which he labeled Lake Ontario Lac St. Louis and sketched in a small river which may have been the Black or the Salmon. A 1688 map by Father Raffiex traced a slight indentation on Black River Bay, which he called Niaourne. Guy Johnson, in his map of 1771, drew in a short, unlabeled river flowing into what he marked Niourne Bay. Sauthier's map, printed in England in 1777, and considered the last word in map-making, failed to show the Black River, and the North Country bore the inscription: "This marshy tract is full of beavers and otters."

This ignorance of the Black River existed as late as 1796, when Jedediah Morse, the "Father of American Geography,"

17

wrote, in his *Universal American Geography:* "Black River rises in the high country, near the sources of Canada Creek which falls into Mohawk River, and takes its course northwest and then northeast till it discharges itself into Cataraqua or Iroquois River not far from Swegauchee. It is said to be navigable for batteaux up to the lower falls, 60 miles, which is distant from the flourishing settlement of Whitestown 25 miles. The whole distance of this river is reckoned at 112 miles." Morse's map was quite accurate in relation to the Lake Champlain, Mohawk River and St. Lawrence–Lake Ontario regions, but it showed the same colossal ignorance betrayed by its predecessors as far as the Black River was concerned. Nwernois Bay (Black River Bay) appeared, inaccurately drawn, and what Morse considered the course of the Black River, but did not label as such, showed a river flowing north through "Oswigatchie River and Lake" to the St. Lawrence River at a point near present Ogdensburg. The North Country above "Stuben" was labeled "McComb's Purchase."

Though Morse's spelling was primitive, he evidently was aware of Baron Frederick William von Steuben's tract on the heights overlooking Remsen, and he also knew that one Alexander Macomb had purchased most of the North Country.

Macomb was the most flamboyant of a group of three wealthy Irishman from New York City who made this purchase. He had come to this country in 1751 with his father at the age of five. As a young man, he had travelled to Detroit and had engaged in the fur trade with John Jacob Astor. Of the three purchasers, he was the only one familiar with the North Country, for his trips along the Great Lakes and the St. Lawrence River had brought him close to the so-called "waste lands" at the mouth of the Black River.

William Constable had been brought to New York in 1761 by his father, a British army surgeon who had been assigned to duty in that city. The younger Constable engaged in the mercantile business, particularly in overseas trade, and may have been the first man to send trading ships to China.

Daniel McCormick, a poor immigrant boy, made a fortune in the mercantile business and served as one of the first directors of the Bank of New York. He was a bachelor whose style of dress did not progress with the times, for he appeared in knee-breeches, white stockings, buckled shoes and powdered hair long after this fashion had become outmoded.

These three men purchased all of what are now Lewis and Jefferson Counties, plus holdings in St. Lawrence and Oswego Counties, a total of nearly four million acres. The price? Eight pence an acre. The first patents were issued in 1792, and others in 1795 and 1798.

The tract became known as the Macomb Purchase, though Macomb may have been a front for Constable and McCormick, and his participation was but for six months. He was a man of grandiose schemes. The ink was scarcely dry on the first patent papers when he got involved in the Company of the Million Bank of the State of New York, which collapsed in April. Macomb, completely insolvent, was clapped into jail. Five months later, he turned over to Constable and McCormick his interest in the purchase.

At this point, the scene shifted to France, which was in the midst of a bloody revolution. Lands of the aristocrats were being confiscated. Powdered heads fell under the guillotine. The king and queen languished in a prison from which they would not emerge alive.

A wealthy Frenchman, Jacques Donatien Le Ray de Chaumont, had not only entertained Benjamin Franklin and John Paul Jones at his mansion at Passy, near Paris on the road to Versailles, but had provided money and ships to aid the American Revolution. After the war, Congress showed no inclination to repay, so Jacques Le Ray sent his son, James Donatien Le Ray de Chaumont, to collect these debts. James Le Ray spent five years in America, during which time he cleared up much of the financial difficulties, married an American girl, and became an American citizen.

William Constable, through Governeur Morris, had met

James Le Ray, who had returned to France to salvage what he could of his family property from the greedy grasp of the French revolutionists. It occurred to Constable that thousands of frightened French aristocrats needed a haven from the storm that was destroying them. He could not only save them; he could dispose of vast plots of land in the Macomb Purchase.

Constable sailed for France, in August, 1792, to see James Le Ray. He did not find him at Passy, for that mansion had been lost to the revolutionists. He located Le Ray at Château de Chaumont sur Loire, the turreted family château which had been built in 940 between Blois and Tours.

James Le Ray had saved the château through a shrewd maneuver. The French revolutionists, despite their antipathy for aristocrats, had great respect for their fellow republicans across the Atlantic, and they revered that grand old man, Benjamin Franklin. It is said that Franklin suggested the solution to the Le Rays' problem. James Le Ray was an American citizen. American property was under the protection of French law. James Le Ray had his father sign over Château de Chaumont sur Loire to him, and the family home was safe until the end of the French Revolution.

James Le Ray showed interest in Constable's plan of salvation for the French aristocrats. He owned land near Cooperstown, where Judge William Cooper, father of the novelist, acted as his land agent. He had heard accounts of the Black River country, chiefly from Governeur Morris, who was to gain considerable wealth from land sales there, and was to have a village named after him.

Drawn into the picture was Le Ray's brother-in-law, M. Pierre Chassanis, and it was Chassanis who signed an agreement with Constable to become proprietor, together with a group of French aristocrats, of 630,000 acres in the North Country, extending from the High Falls to Lake Ontario. The price was to be £52,000. Chassanis organized La Compagnie de New York but, by the end of the year, did not get enough subscribers. Constable, the shrewd businessman, cancelled the agreement and awaited developments. By April, 1793, he was able to sell Chassanis 215,000 acres for £25,000.

The new venture bore the name Castorland Company and its capital was to be the inland city of Castorville, a new Paris. French aristocrats would come to vast estates, where they would build noble châteaux and conduct hunts day after day in the virgin forest. Sales from lumber, potash and maple sugar would make each man rich. Boats would sail down the Black River to Lake Ontario, where a great seaport, the City of Basle, would form a connecting link with the mother country. All seemed rosy, indeed.

Inasmuch as William Constable died without seeing the North Country, he must have been using his imagination while luring Le Ray, Chassanis and the aristocrats. The map he showed probably was that of Sauthier, which proved that Castorland lay in the same latitude with southern France, a land of vineyards and fruit trees. One wonders if Constable knew about, or revealed to the desperate Frenchmen, the fact that the year-round climate of the Black River region varied considerably from that along the shores of the Mediterranean Sea.

Constable was familiar with the Sauthier map and its inaccuracies, for he wrote to a prospective buyer, Patrick Colquhoun, in 1792: "Mr. Sauthier in forming this map must have gone on the vague information of the Indians who you know are incapable of conceiving a geographical idea or of conveying exact information as to the extent of swamps, or situations, distances, &c.

"As proof that this country was never explored Mr. Sauthier in his maps, takes not the least notice of the Black River, although it runs for a certainty, about 60 miles through the tract marked off by Colonel Smith and Judge Cooper, who purchased Noble's tract, in which this river takes its rise, proposed making a large purchase of the proprietors who refused to sell, and Mr. Cockburn, the surveyor who explored this river, states nothing about swamps, but gives a very favorable account indeed, of the country, and as a proof of this good opinion of the soil and its situation, he was desirous of buying a large tract within the bounds marked off by Colonel Smith."

This was the Brantingham Tract in Lewis County, which was sold to William Inman in trust for Colquhoun in 1793. William Cockburn & Son of Poughkeepsie (some say Kingston) had surveyed the 16,000 acres of Baron Steuben. John Cockburn, who did this job, reached the heights above Remsen by a water route, via the Hudson and Mohawk Rivers, the West Canada Creek and the Cincinnati Creek. With five other surveyors, he completed the survey between April and October, 1787. The Cockburns had been engaged by Constable to survey the borders of the Macomb Purchase and it is evident from Constable's letter to Colquhoun that they were on the job in 1792.

The Castorland Company, with commissioners in Paris, including Chassanis and James Le Ray, decided to send two men to this new Utopia to inspect the land and prepare it for the flood of émigrés who would tax the trans-Atlantic ships for years to come. The men chosen were M. Pierre Pharoux, a prominent young Parisian architect, and M. Simon Desjardines, who had gained a reputation as an adventurer.

Pharoux and Desjardines landed in New York on September 7, 1793. Desjardines brought along his wife and children, his brother, and his library of 2,000 volumes. By the 27th, Pharoux and the brothers Desjardines were in Schenectady. A surveyor, M. Marc Isambard Brunel, had been engaged in Albany.

These Frenchmen chose not to plunge directly into the northern wilderness. They went by batteaux up the Mohawk River to Fort Stanwix, crossed the Carrying Place to Wood Creek, poled their way down that stream to Oneida Lake and followed the Oswego River to Lake Ontario. At Oswego, they engaged a small sailboat, which carried them to Henderson Harbor.

On October 20th, after some difficulty, they located the mouth of the Black River, which they found to be unnavigable, so they set out on foot for Castorland. They fought their way through the wilderness as far as the Great Falls (Watertown) and young M. Pharoux, impressed by the surge of coffee-colored water, hardly realized that he was to meet his doom there less than two years later. Cold nights presaged the onrush of winter, so the Frenchmen retraced their route and returned to Albany.

The following May 18th found the two Desjardines, Brunel and a M. Quernel at Old Fort Schuyler (Utica), where they were met by M. Pharoux. The Frenchmen had heard of Baron Steuben's colony in the wilderness, so they decided to go there over a rude road the Baron had constructed. They arrived at Steuben's Sixty Acres to learn that the general was not at home. Undaunted, Pharoux and three surveyors attacked the wilderness to open up a road Steuben had started toward the north. Desjardines followed with a wagon loaded with supplies. Pharoux may have hired Steuben settlers for the road project, for 26 men were engaged in this undertaking.

The party reached the High Falls (Lyons Falls) and began to construct two log cabins on the east bank of the Black River below the falls. Workmen also busied themselves building a canoe.

Here Desjardines made a shocking discovery. The land sold to Chassanis by William Constable was not as represented. The French purchasers had been under the impression that the river flowed west; instead, its course was north to the great bend. As a result, the French holdings lay to the east of the river, except for a narrow strip north of the great bend to Lake Ontario. Desjardines hurried to New York to have a talk with James Constable, who was acting as land agent for his brother. Desjardines got little satisfaction. In answer to his complaint that French land owners could not go from one estate to another without going outside their property, Constable said he could not change the course of the river.

Desjardines, disappointed and unhappy, hastened back to Old Fort Schuyler, where he received the news that the whole party at the High Falls was sick. He rode horseback over the crude roads to the new colony. Discouragement faced him. Pharoux was ill and several men had died. Desjardines also sickened, so he and Pharoux had but one choice, to abandon the project and try again the next spring. Another blow hit the bedraggled party when it reached Steuben. The Baron had died and had been buried in his military cape in a lonely spot beside the road they had labored so hard to build.

Desjardines did not down easily. He and Pharoux were back at the High Falls in the spring of 1795. For the first time, they made progress. Rude mills were constructed at the High Falls and the Long Falls.

Tragedy struck again. Pharoux was travelling down river with a party of surveyors led by Charles C. Brodhead, whose job it was to survey and subdivide the land into plots of 50 acres. The party had crossed and recrossed the river several times in improvised rafts. One day, they came to the bank of the river at a place Brodhead thought he recognized, so they built a raft and poled it out into the stream. Suddenly, without warning, they heard the roar of the Great Falls. Their poles failed to find bottom, and Brodhead realized he had chosen the wrong crossing and they were at the head of the rapids leading to the Great Falls. He ordered all who could swim to jump into the river and strike out for shore. Pharoux could not swim, so Brodhead, a strong swimmer, chose to stay on the raft with his French friend and other non-swimmers. The raft rushed through the rapids and was hurtled over the falls, where it was shattered. Brodhead was thrown into an eddy, from which he swam to shore. Pharoux and several other men were drowned. The body of the Frenchman was found on the shore of an island near Dexter by Benjamin Wright, another surveyor, and given a decent burial.

Desjardines left two families to winter in Castorland, but they could not endure the severe weather. They came out in February, driving cattle ahead of them.

The spring of 1796 found Desjardines back at the High Falls for another try. In travelling down the river, he could not forget that Pharoux had named the Independence River in honor of American independence and had chosen a beautiful spot near its mouth for his home in America. Desjardines recorded in his diary, on May 18th: "Landed at half-past two at Independence Rock, and visited once more this charming spot which had been so beautifully chosen by our friend Pharoux as the site for his house. The azaleas in full bloom loaded the air with their perfume, and the wild birds sang sweetly around their nests, but nature has no longer any pleasant sights, nor fragrance, nor music, for me."

This was Desjardines' swan song, for M. Rudolphe Tillier appeared to give him the news that he had been replaced. Desjardines returned to France and never set eyes on the Black River again.

Brodhead's attempt to save Pharoux, and the burial of the Frenchman's body by Benjamin Wright, bring to the fore a group of men who were the unsung heroes of the struggle to open up the Black River wilderness. Regional histories mention them as having surveyed town boundaries and having divided towns into plots. Otherwise, they have been ignored, though without their efforts settlement would have been long delayed.

The earliest surveyors to attack the wilderness above the Mohawk Valley were William Cockburn & Son and Calvin Guiteau of Deerfield. John Cockburn surveyed Steuben's 16,000 acres. Guiteau, who surveyed much of the land in Oneida County north of Old Fort Schuyler, also did considerable work in the town of Ellisburg.

The Cockburns, in surveying the boundaries of the Macomb Purchase, probably were the men who discovered that the Black River did not flow in the direction indicated by

William Constable. They completed their survey to Lake Ontario in 1799, after at least seven years of hard work.

Brodhead's job was to divide the Chassanis purchase into lots for sale. He also surveyed "Inman's Triangle," which included the towns of Lewis and Leyden in Lewis County, for William Inman of Utica, the father of two sons who became famous: William rose to the rank of commodore in the United States Navy; Henry became the foremost American landscape and portrait painter of his day. And it was Brodhead who produced the first accurate map of the Black River country. This map, printed at the close of his surveying operations around 1800, showed the Black River flowing as it does at the present time, and emptying into what he labeled "Hungary Bay," a variation of Hungry Bay which indicates that he thought Black River Bay was Hungry Bay.

While Brodhead was dividing the Chassanis purchase into plots, Benjamin Wright and his brother, Moses, from Wright Settlement near Rome, were surveying the "Eleven Towns" for various proprietors who, having bought land in the Macomb Purchase, were dividing it into townships and into plots for sale by their land agents.

These "Eleven Towns," with their numbers, original names and present names in parentheses, were: 1. Hesiod (Hounsfield) 2. Leghorn (Watertown) 3. Milan (Rutland) 4. Howard (Champion) 5. Mantua (Denmark) 6. Henderson (Henderson) 7. Aleppo (Adams) 8. Orpheus (Rodman) 9. Fenelon (Worth and Pinckney) 10. Handel (Harrisburg) and 11. Lowville (Lowville). Towns 1, 4, 5, 8 and 10 were owned by Richard Harrison and J. O. Hoffman; Richard Henderson purchased towns 3, 6 and 9; Nicholas Low bought towns 2 and 11. The classical influence, which extended to towns in Lewis County, was erased on April 6, 1808, when the towns received their present names.

The Wrights kept accurate accounts of their surveys and added prophetic comments about the potentialities of each town. They noted the harbor facilities of Henderson and

Hounsfield, the water power for mill sites at Watertown and Champion, and the agricultural resources of Adams, Champion, Denmark, Lowville and Watertown. They considered Rodman and Rutland pretty good country, but thought little of Harrisburg and Pinckney, claiming that the latter town was "cold and hemlocky." In surveying Henderson, they located it "along Hungry Bay," indicating that they, like Brodhead, thought that place to be near the Black River and not at the Salmon River.

Brodhead was but 21 and Benjamin Wright 25 when they went to survey the North Country, a job which utilized their talents for nearly ten years. Brodhead later surveyed the line of the Erie Canal from Albany to Utica. Wright not only surveyed, but constructed the section from Utica to Rome. The two surveyors united their efforts in 1812, when they traced a route for the unsuccessful St. Lawrence Turnpike through the town of Diana.

These early surveying parties, usually consisting of a handful of men, ventured into unknown territory and endured hardship in order to survey the land. Dr. Hough paid Benjamin Wright this tribute: "For weeks in succession, his parties pitched their tents in the trackless forests, far from the habitations of white men,—the form of the savage the only one encountered by day, and the fierce wolf and panther hovering around them at night, kept at bay only by their circling fires. With steady and indomitable industry he pursued his way, deterred by no difficulty, when in the performance of his engagements."

To go back to the French attempt at settlement, M. Tillier tried to encourage aristocrats to come to Castorland, but he fought a losing battle. More Frenchmen were returning to the mother country than were emigrating to Castorland.

A few non-French settlers made a go of pioneering along the Black River and its tributaries. A letter, written in English, was washed up on the coast of Denmark after the wreck of the "Morning Star" in 1800. It had been written by a settler on the "pretty Beaver River" at a place known as "Castor-ville." The writer mentioned that there were several primitive dwellings at the settlement, including a store, and that the inhabitants were mostly Scotch and Irish. The most tantalizing sentences read: "Our rivers abound in fish, and our brooks in trout. I have seen two men take 72 in a day."

Despite this encouraging letter, the Castorland Company's settlements were considered failures. By 1804, there was nothing at the High Falls and but one filthy tavern at the Long Falls.

Judged in terms of physical achievement, the attempt of the French aristocrats to conquer the Black River region was not a success. And yet, it must be remembered that the first true knowledge of the North Country was gained through this attempt, and that this information was put to good use by the more practical Yankees who succeeded where the impractical French aristocrats had failed.

IV

YANKEE PIONEERS

THE SEEDS for a permanent settlement of the Black River region were being sown while the refugees from the French Revolution were blundering, suffering and dying at the High Falls. Available land was scarce in New England, so many veterans of the American Revolution and their sons migrated to the Mohawk Valley shortly after the war. While there, they learned about the fabulous territory from the High Falls to Lake Ontario, where land was so fertile that wheat would yield 25 to 30 bushels to the acre and corn would grow to a height of eleven feet. Virgin forests of oak, elm, beech, hickory and basswood waited to provide wood for cabins and mills. Trees and brush, when burned in clearing land, would produce potash, a valuable commodity which found a ready market in Montreal and Quebec. And there was always the Black River, open to navigation from the High Falls to the Long Falls, and available for water power above and below these points.

The stream of settlement, which had confined itself to the east-west routes of the Mohawk and the St. Lawrence, added a new course, north from the Mohawk Valley through the Black River country to Lake Ontario. Baron Steuben's colony, which included many Welsh, started the tide of settlers northward. The French experiment gave it an impetus. The Holland Land Company, through its first agent, Gerrit Boon, established settlements at Oldenbarneveld and Boonville. And, up near the Sugar River in the town of Leyden, William Topping of Meriden, Conn., with his wife and two small children, was living in a leanto a month before Desjardines and Pharoux cut the French Road through to the High Falls in the spring of 1794. By the close of the next year, ten families from Connecticut were putting up cabins in what is now the town of Leyden.

These early settlers may have received information about the Black River country from Charles C. Brodhead, who had been surveying Inman's Triangle. And it was he who directed the first settlers to Lowville in the spring of 1797. Four men from Westfield, Mass. had gone on a tour of inspection of the Genesee country but had returned as far as Whitestown, for they had found the western lands "too sickly." Here they ran into Brodhead, who traced a route for them to Leyden, where Silas Stow, agent for Nicholas Low, was making his headquarters. They followed the line of blazings on the trees and Stow took them to what is now Lowville, where they purchased land at three dollars an acre. After putting up rude huts, they returned to Westfield for the winter.

In early spring, 1798, a party of 14 people left Westfield and reached the High Falls in late March, after a rough trip through the wilderness. In the group were Jonathan Rogers and his three children; Ehud Stephens, with his wife and three children; Jesse Wilcox, Zebulon Rogers, Philemon Hoadley and the Woolworth brothers, Elijah and Justus. Ice still encased the Black River, so the Westfield men borrowed tools from the French émigrés and built a flat-bottomed boat 25 feet long and seven feet wide, the largest craft to float on the river up to that time. On April 10th, the ice having broken, they loaded the boat with household goods, provisions and their families, until its gunwales were scarcely two inches above water. Their French friends towed the boat into the swollen river, where it got caught in an eddy and was nearly swept beneath the falls. Desperate rowing guided it near shore. Two young men, Bela Rogers and Justus Woolworth, jumped into the water with a tow line and the boat was steered to the French settlement, where much of its load was removed. This precaution paid off, for the boat, with its provisions and passengers, floated down the swollen river without mishap to the mouth of Lowville (Mill) Creek. Here the men got into the water and pushed the loaded craft up the creek. Clarissa Rogers caused moments of anxiety when an overhanging tree brushed her off the boat, but she was soon rescued. The journey came to a halt when the boat got marooned on a tree which had fallen across the creek, so the boat was dislodged and brought to shore.

By this time, the sun was setting, but Rogers and Woolworth set out in search of the rude cabins which had been put up the previous summer. Darkness fell, and they did not return to the anxious group huddled on the shore. Suddenly, a bright light shone through the trees. The young men had located the cabins and had built a huge bonfire to attract the attention of their friends and relatives. With the aid of the light, and occasional toots on hunting horns, the party reached the cabins, where they cooked and ate a hearty meal and bedded down for the night.

The next few days were spent in reconditioning the cabins

and in making trips to the High Falls for the rest of the supplies and to Turin to drive in cattle which had been left at the last clearing. Philemon Hoadley and the Woolworth brothers did not return to Lowville, for they had decided to locate in the town of Turin.

Dr. Hough tells a story about the pair of domestic fowl the Rogers family brought with them. It was not long before the rooster and hen became parents of a brood of chickens. One day, while the hen was clucking to her offspring, a hawk swooped down and carried her away. Old Logan, the rooster, thinking that his race faced extermination unless he did something to prevent it, guarded and sheltered the chickens until they reached maturity.

Baron Steuben's settlement around Sixty Acres had attracted a considerable number of settlers with adventuresome spirits. Capt. Simeon Woodruff had been a midshipman with Capt. Cook when the latter had been killed by natives in the Sandwich Islands. Capt. David Starr had served seven years in the Continental army and was a member of the Order of the Cincinnati, a society for officers which the Baron had been instrumental in founding. Starr, the father of 12 children, came from Middletown, Conn. As a farmer, he proved to be a rank failure and could not keep up his payments on the land. After Steuben's death in 1794, Col. Benjamin Walker of Utica, who was handling the Baron's estate, pressed Starr for long overdue payments. Starr's dignity was hurt, so he responded by challenging Walker to a duel over the Baron's grave, claiming that a comrade-in-arms like Walker should not embarrass an old soldier. Walker wisely withdrew his suit.

Among the younger settlers on Steuben's land was Noadiah Hubbard, who had come up from Whitestown in 1792. Hubbard, like Starr, was from Middletown, Conn. He had gone to sea as a boy and had made several trips in sailing ships to the West Indies. While in Whitestown, he had manufactured the first brick and had burned the first lime made and used in that settlement. In 1794, he was in charge of building the canal locks at Little Falls for the Western Inland Navigation Company. He considered himself well-paid for this job, for he received a dollar a day for his services.

Lemuel Storrs of Middletown had purchased extensive tracts of land in what is now the town of Champion. He knew Hubbard, so he asked him to go along to take a look at the land. In late autumn of 1797, when Hubbard was 32 years of age, the two Connecticut Yankees travelled by foot along the French Road to the High Falls, where a huddle of log huts marked the colony at that place. Here they ran into Silas Stow, the land agent. The three men took a boat down the river to the Long Falls, where Storrs and Hubbard plunged into the wilderness. They spent two days inspecting the land, and Hubbard was impressed by what he saw.

The return trip involved hazards. The Black River in November flowed cold and swift, so it took the three men two days to get back to the High Falls, where they were overtaken by snow and a lack of provisions. Hubbard had shot a duck and a partridge on the way up the river. The men built a leanto covered with hemlock boughs and fell into a sleep of exhaustion. In the morning, Hubbard cooked the duck and the partridge, using, in the absence of salt, the few pieces of salt pork he had left, to stuff the fowl. This sumptuous meal eaten, the men took the French Road back to Steuben.

When Hubbard talked during the winter of moving to Champion, Capt. Starr probably would have been delighted to go along, but he was 60 years old. David, Jr. had turned 21. He was an unlettered young man who thrived on wilderness life and possessed the adventurous spirit of his father. Hubbard decided to take him and young Simeon Ward to Champion. Hubbard had to make a hard choice. His holdings in Steuben were successful and he had been elected supervisor of the town. Moving to Champion meant more back-breaking labor; but, when he thought of the fertile land and the abundant forests, he decided to go.

The three young men left Steuben on June 1, 1798, taking

with them supplies to be shipped down the Black River from the High Falls, driving ahead of them fifteen head of cattle. After leaving the supplies at the High Falls, they travelled by land to Hoadley's (Collinsville), where they met Benjamin Wright and a group of surveyors who were mapping out a route to Hounsfield. Wright left them at Shaler's (Turin) and went ahead, marking trees so that the men from Steuben could follow. Hubbard lost the blazes on the trees, so he consulted a rude map and decided to take as direct a course as possible, over what is now Tug Hill. Night fell, so the men camped under a leanto of hemlock boughs.

A council took place in the morning. The land through which they had passed the day before had been filled with gulleys, and passage of the cattle had been difficult. Unknown territory lay ahead. If Hubbard returned, he would suffer a severe loss. He asked his companions if they were willing to go on.

David Starr was a chip off the old block. He settled the issue by saying, "I'll go to hell, if you will."

They went on. One man drove the cattle, while a second man marked trees, so that they could return in case they became lost. They struck the Deer River not far from what is now the village of Copenhagen and followed the Champion line markings to the Long Falls, arriving before nightfall.

Wright and his surveyors had come in an hour earlier. Wright exclaimed, "How, in the name of God, have you got here!"

Hubbard, thoroughly angry, retorted, "You scoundrel! You ought to be burnt for leaving us so."

The boat from the High Falls arrived, with yokes, chains, cooking utensils, etc. One man guarded these valuables, while the other two searched for a desirable location. Hubbard selected his plot and lived on it to the end of his long life. In his eighty-ninth year, he wrote to Dr. Hough, describing his experiences and boasting, "I was the *first* settler in the (Jefferson) county."

The men spent the summer in finding a spring, making a clearing, building a rude cabin and a bake oven and planting some potatoes. They returned to Steuben in the autumn, driving ahead of them fattened cattle.

Hubbard sent two men ahead in the spring of 1799 to make maple sugar. They discovered that Indians had stolen the cooking utensils, also potatoes Hubbard had buried. These sugar-makers got an urge to go hunting. They left the sap boiling in a vat inside the cabin and went into the forest. On their return, the cabin was a smouldering heap of embers.

Hubbard arrived in late spring, bringing with him ten young men from Steuben and Henry Boutin, who became the first settler at what is now Carthage. Lemuel Storrs failed financially that year. Hubbard, knowing he could not stand losing the land he had cleared nor the money he had paid Storrs, brought his wife and small children to Champion in the fall. Eunice Hubbard, the ideal pioneer wife, chose to walk the four miles from the Long Falls to the Hubbard clearing, saying, "If I have anything as good as a cave to live in, I will not return in a year at least." The Hubbards spent the winter in a cabin almost buried with snow. They were comfortable, and they knew the time of day, for they owned the first clock made in what is now Utica and the first in the North Country. It had no case, and was fastened to a wall of the cabin.

Whatever loneliness they may have encountered during the winter was dissipated in the spring, when settlers coming to the North Country used Hubbard's cabin for a temporary inn. At times the floor was so thickly strewn with sleeping pioneers that some had to lie too close to the huge fireplace and as a result were considerably toasted.

Hubbard lived to see his settlement grow. The soil was good, and the majority of the settlers were interested in agriculture. Hubbard became the bulwark of his community: he was the first supervisor of the town of Champion and a trustee of the first school; he built the first church, mostly at his own expense; he served as a captain in the War of 1812 and was active in getting better roads for the town.

David Starr took a trip to New Haven, Conn. and brought back a wife who taught the backwoods boy to read and to write. Starr became a solid citizen, owning and managing a farm, a grist mill, the village store and a distillery. Later, he moved to Adams. Old Capt. Starr, on a visit to his son, died in Adams and is buried there. His name is left for posterity on one of the highest points in Oneida County, the towering mass known as Starr Hill, on the slope of which he had cleared land purchased from Baron Steuben.

Pioneers from Massachusetts and Connecticut had pushed the frontier from the Mohawk Valley to Champion. A Quaker from Bucks County, Pennsylvania, was to extend it to Lake Ontario. Jacob Brown, who had left home to teach school in New York City, had made the acquaintance of Governeur Morris, who introduced him to M. Rudolphe Tillier, agent for Chassanis. Tillier sold Brown's father a large tract of land for two dollars an acre. Jacob Brown, not yet 24 years of age, reached the High Falls in March, 1799 with two companions and some hired men. He too had to wait for the ice to break before floating down the Black River to the Long Falls in a boat. After following a crude road M. Tillier had cut along the east bank of the river, Brown arrived at the mouth of Philomel Creek, where he chose his land. His father and the rest of the Brown family came via Oswego later in the spring, and all of the Browns got to work to clear land, raise cabins and build mills at what was to be Brownville.

If Brown had stayed a little longer at the High Falls, he might have met Henry and David Coffeen, Vermonters who had been living a few years in the town of Schuyler in the Mohawk Valley. They too took the river route to the Long Falls and tramped through the wilderness on the west side of the river to the town of Rutland, where David purchased 391 acres from Silas Stow. Henry went on to the Great Falls and bought, also from Stow, 220 acres bordering the Black River and extending toward Brownville.

The Coffeens brought their families up from Schuyler in the spring of 1800. Henry chose to come through the wilderness from Lowville. The ox-sled carrying his furniture and provisions had such a rough passage that most of the furniture was in splinters when it reached the Great Falls.

Zachariah Butterfield arrived from Schuyler that summer, as did Deacon Oliver Bartholomew, who chose his land between the Great Falls and Brownville. The Massey brothers, Hart and Dr. Isaiah, walked all the way over from Vermont to purchase land at the Great Falls. New Hampshire entered the competition with Abraham and Nathan Jewett, who arrived with an ox team, two barrels of pork and a barrel of meal.

One of Noadiah Hubbard's visitors at Champion was young Jonathan Baker, a teamster who was following the Jewett brothers to the new settlement at the Great Falls. Baker spent the night with the Hubbards. At sunrise, on a February morning, he started out on foot along a blind sled path. The way was so poorly marked and he was in such unfamiliar territory, that darkness caught up with him before he reached his destination. He sat down to rest and fell asleep. When he awoke, the moon was shining down on the surrounding forest, and a feeling of great loneliness swept over him. The chill air roused him to action and, by the light of the moon, he kept walking until his ears caught the roar of a great cataract. A light appeared ahead. It shone from the cabin of Henry Coffeen.

Mrs. Coffeen must have been surprised when Baker appeared at her door in the middle of the night, but she invited him in. She apologized for lack of food, for she and the children had eaten the last of the supply for supper, and her husband was on his way back from Whitestown, where he had walked to replenish the family larder. She recalled that Zachariah Butterfield had returned with supplies that afternoon, so she went to the Butterfield cabin and borrowed pork, which she fried, and meal, which she made into a cake. After he had eaten, Baker lay down on the floor and fell asleep.

Walking seemed to be the chief activity of these pioneers. Henry Coffeen's trip to Whitestown was "mere punkins" compared to the hike Baker made back to New Hampshire later in the year to get some clothes and to bring back eight more settlers.

Sawmills and gristmills were the pressing need of the early settlers in Watertown. Sandy Creek was considered more suited to the purpose than the powerful river, and it was on Sandy Creek that a sawmill and a corn mill were built by Hart Massey in June, 1801. Silas Stow, who had sold the settlers the land, paid for the irons, millstones, etc. The mills were sold to John Burr, after whom Burrville was named.

Mills went up along the Black River and its tributaries. David Coffeen built one at the Long Falls and threw a crude dam across the river. He also built a gristmill at the mouth of Mill Creek at Felts Mills. A sawmill was put into operation at Great Bend. Lowville had a sawmill as early as 1798 on Mill Creek. A gristmill followed in the next year. Jacob Brown built mills at Brownville on Philomel Creek. Gen. Walter Martin started a sawmill and a gristmill at Martinsburg. And so it went, up and down the river and its tributaries.

Stores were also necessary. Samuel Brown operated one in Brownville; David Starr kept store at Champion; Fortunatus Eager opened a store in Lowville. Cape Vincent had two, owned by J. B. & R. M. Esselstyn and Dr. Avery Ainsworth. Henry Coffeen, tiring of the trips to Lowville and Whitestown, induced Amasa Fox to build a store in Watertown. Before the building was finished, Mrs. Coffeen and two other ladies were doing some quilting there. A spark from the pipe of a girl named Andrus fell into the shavings and the store was burned. It wasn't until 1805 that Watertown could boast a store, owned by William Smith and Capt. John Paddock.

Taverns were necessities along the route to the North Country. The Hoadleys at Collinsville catered to pioneers, as did William Holliday at Turin, Eleazer House at Houseville, David Waters at Martinsburg and Jonathan Rogers at Lowville. Levi Butterfield entertained guests at Rutland Center, Isaac Massey built the first tavern in Watertown, and Jean Baptiste Bossuot, a native of France, kept what travellers described as a "very filthy place" at the Long Falls.

Freedom Wright's tavern at Denmark was destined to play a prominent part in the history of the North Country, for it was there that the representatives of the towns met on Nov. 20, 1804 to consider the separation of the Black River valley from Oneida County and the establishment of a new county and county seat. Thirty-six men attended. They voted to part company with Oneida County and to form, not one, but two new counties, which were to be named Lewis, after Governor Morgan Lewis of New York, and Jefferson, after Thomas Jefferson, the President of the United States. Champion was disappointed, for it had advocated but one county and had desired the county seat. Lowville also suffered a setback when it lost the county seat of Lewis to Martinsburg. Jacob Brown left with a bitter taste in his mouth when the county seat for Jefferson was assigned to Henry Coffeen's Watertown.

For a county seat, Watertown wasn't much of a place. Harry F. Landon described it: "Let no one get the idea that Watertown in this day was a cozy, rustic village. On the contrary, it was crude, unkempt and unlovely. Most of the 17 or 18 little huts were of logs and of what we would call today temporary construction. Within the next few years, they would be largely replaced by frame, stone or brick structures. The forest was everywhere and stumps stood in the clearings. The hollow maple stump, in which the first settlers ground their corn, still stood in front of Massey's log inn although by now most of the pioneers took their corn to Burr's mill at the present Burrville. By 1805, the little hotel, long known as the White House, had been constructed on the site of the present Woolworth Building but a sketch preserved at the Jefferson

Brownville Bridge and Mills, 1815, from etching by French artist, Jacques Milbert. Courtesy of Jefferson County Historical Society.

Noadiah Hubbard House at Champion, still standing, built in 1831. Photo by David F. Lane.

Le Ray Mansion, Le Raysville. Built between 1825 and 1827. Photo by David F. Lane.

County Historical Society's museum shows that this was simply a square, unattractive house with the word, 'Hotel,' painted on its side."

Unlovely or not, Watertown got William Smith to build a combination courthouse and jail. The superintendents were empowered "to build a sufficient tower and cupola on the centre of said building, and cover the dome of said cupola with tin, and so construct said tower and cupola that it shall be sufficiently strong and convenient so as to hang a bell, and erect a sphere and vane, and also a suitable rod to conduct lightning from said building." This "magnificent" building, with all its frills, burned to the ground on Feb. 9, 1821. In the confusion which followed the fire, Sackets Harbor made a bid for the county seat, but it lost out, and another courthouse and a separate jail were built in Watertown.

The acquisition of the county seat lent prestige to that village. By 1810, its population reached 1,841, edging by about 100 its nearest competitor in Jefferson County, Ellisburg. The Black River had much to do with this rapid development of what had been a backwoods clearing. Henry Coffeen and Andrew Edmonds had built a dam, a mill and a bridge across the river below the Great Falls. Jonathan Cowan, in 1802, built a dam across the river to what was then known as Cowan's Island (Beebee's Island) and put up the first successful sawmill on the Black River. His courage, skill and daring led to the development of water power in Watertown, which began to attract mechanics and men interested in developing industry along the river.

The growth of Watertown from a clearing of three cabins in 1800 to a thriving town with a population of 1,841 in 1810, gives some indication of the wave of migration which was flowing into the North Country during that decade.

The new south-north route through the Black River valley was competing successfully with the east-west routes along the Mohawk and St. Lawrence Rivers. The North Country was no longer "the beaver hunting grounds of the Indians."

V
WAR ALONG THE BORDER

SETTLERS along the Black River had been too busy clearing land, building cabins, raising crops, constructing dams, mills and bridges, and improving roads to pay much attention to what had been transpiring in the country at large. They awoke with a start late in 1807 to learn that the Federal government had placed an embargo on certain articles of exchange with Great Britain. This embargo had the effect of lowering the price of grain, which did not hurt the settlers. Potash was another matter, for sales of that commodity to Canada brought money with which to make payments on land.

Rev. John Taylor, a missionary who visited the Black River country in 1802, reported: "From No. 1 or Brownville, there is a constant trade by boats carried on with Montreal, Kingston and Quebec, principally in flour, pot and pearl ashes. The voyage is performed as far as Kingston in a day—and from Montreal about a week. Business is opening very fast."

The North Country farmers, by ignoring the embargo, could get $300 to $320 per ton for potash delivered at Montreal, from which point it was shipped to England. These settlers considered the risk worth the money. In winter, when the St. Lawrence was frozen over, a number of routes could be taken to Kingston with precious loads of potash. Smugglers usually took the "embargo road" from the Black River to French Creek near Clayton. Hart Massey of Watertown, serving as customs collector of the port of Sackets Harbor, tried to stop the illicit trade by seizing a shipment of potash and pork at Cape Vincent, only to be relieved of his acquisition by 50 or 60 men from Kingston, who took it across the ice on sleds. Militia sent to stop the smuggling were ostracized by the people, who stood in opposition to the embargo, which they claimed was unconstitutional. The smugglers kept up their profitable business right under the noses of the inspectors and the militia, and many a plot of land in the North Country was paid for with money received from the illicit sale of potash.

War with Great Britain had been expected for years, but when the declaration came, on June 18, 1812, the North Country was thrown into a state of panic. Many settlers had come from the Mohawk Valley and the memory of Indian raids still remained fresh in their minds. The people of Antwerp, though well removed from the border, built a blockhouse for protection against Indian attack. The settlers along the Perch River near Brownville did likewise. Their blockhouse was put to use as a storehouse for wheat when the scare subsided. The few families at Cape Vincent, who were engaged in building arks for the Montreal lumber trade, nearly died of fright. Noadiah Hubbard of Champion, who was cutting lumber for rafts on French Creek, suffered a severe loss when one of his rafts was seized and detained by the British at Louisville. And, at the declaration of war, another Hubbard, Abner, no relation, took it upon himself to seize Fort Haldimand on Carleton Island with its garrison of three invalid soldiers and two women. Hubbard's "fleet" consisted of a rowboat and his "army" was composed of himself, a man and a boy. The fort which had defied the Federal government four years earlier thus fell before an amateur force of three.

The focal point of defense of the frontier was Sackets Harbor, manned by militia under Col. Christopher Bellinger from the Mohawk Valley. At the outbreak of war, Jacob Brown of Brownville, a Quaker with some military experience, was authorized to reinforce Bellinger with the militia of Lewis, Jefferson and St. Lawrence counties and to equip them at the State arsenals in Russell and Watertown.

Capt. Noadiah Hubbard and his company from Champion were among the militia called. This company was part of the 26th Brigade of State militia which had been organized in 1805 with Brig. Gen. Walter Martin of Martinsburgh as the commanding officer. The brigade consisted of militia regiments from Lewis and Jefferson counties. These regiments contained from 300–400 men; for example, the 46th Lewis County regiment had 310 men and the 101st Lewis County regiment 367 men. A company from Denmark was with Bellinger's force at Sackets Harbor at the outbreak of the war. Other groups were called to duty as emergencies arose. Some served for but a few days, while others were on duty for six months or more. These militia units were equipped at the new State arsenal, built in Watertown in 1808, though supplies of guns and ammunition were often kept close at hand.

Fortunately for troop movements, the new State Road had been completed from Johnstown to Sackets Harbor and had been joined above Remsen by a new highway from Utica. It was over this "Military Road" that the militia from several states marched to the defense of the frontier. Utica was the congregating point for militia going to and from Sackets Harbor. The troops scarcely were a hit in the first-named village, for they were for the most part dirty, foul-mouthed and undisciplined. Here are a few comments on them: a company of flying artillery from Pennsylvania was "very dirty, and brown as Indians, variously dressed, most of them young, and largely made up of foreigners;" Gen. Dodge's army of regulars and militia from Albany were "young and able-bodied, but undisciplined and unmanageable;" the soldiers of the 5th United States Regiment of regulars were "dirty, saucy to their officers and clamorous for their pay, which was six months overdue;" a regiment from Massachusetts was "opposed to the invasion of Canada and generally discontented."

The regiments described were probably typical of the outfits which fought during the war. Folks living on or near the Military Road became accustomed to seeing troops pass, either to or from the scene of military action. Bands of sailors were common, and one group of 100 was assigned to the famous "U.S.S. Constitution." British prisoners were taken down the Military Road; one outfit was described as "a fine body of men, some of them being over six feet in height." Strange to say, most of these prisoners spoke German and French. These troop movements lent a touch of color and excitement to the drab lives of settlers in the Black River valley, who went out of their way at first to provide comforts for the soldiers, but later learned to guard their orchards, gardens and hen-roosts, for the passing troops showed no respect for personal property of others.

The British waited but a month before making a move against Sackets Harbor. At dawn on Sunday morning, July 19th, 1812, Gen. Jacob Brown heard cannon booming at the Harbor and recognized this pre-arranged signal. He gathered his militia, packed them into large wagons drawn by farm horses, and rushed them pell-mell to the scene of action.

The only ship the Americans owned at the Harbor was the "Oneida," commanded by Melancthon Taylor Woolsey, who knew his vessel was too slow to elude the British ships, so he anchored her off shore, unloaded her guns, brought them to land and stationed them in positions to rake the British ships if they came within range. Gen. Brown and his militia arrayed themselves on the plateau later occupied by Madison Barracks. Brown boasted one cannon, a short, fat thirty-two which had been captured by Ethan Allen at Fort Ticonderoga in the early years of the American Revolution. The men called it "Old Sow."

When Woolsey refused a British demand to surrender, the British flagship, the "Royal George," opened fire on the American defenses. "Old Sow" tried to respond, but only twenty-four-pound balls were available. The expedient of wrapping the balls in pieces of carpets and petticoats supplied by the women of the village failed.

Crowds from the surrounding countryside had gathered to

witness the battle, for this was the big event in the lives of the people.

Woolsey's cannon engaged in an ineffectual duel with the "Royal George." Shots taken by British gunners at Brown's militia fell short. The British were firing thirty-two-pound balls. One plowed into the plateau within reach of a Yankee militiaman, who promptly rescued it. A sergeant rammed it into "Old Sow" and cried, "We've ketched 'em out now, boys! Let's send it back!"

"Old Sow" responded with a sharp pop. The ball, accurately aimed, tore a mast off the "Royal George" and injured some of its crew. The flagship, damaged by its own ammunition, gave the signal to withdraw. "Old Sow" had saved the day.

The crowd cheered lustily, but most folks were a bit disappointed at the British withdrawal. As one man expressed it, "All the British broke was the Sabbath."

Black River settlements got a thrill the following winter, when Gen. Zebulon Pike and a regiment of regulars marched through in bitter-cold weather, the men on snowshoes and bundled to their necks in greatcoats. At Watertown, Pike's soldiers hung up 500 pairs of snowshoes on a wall in the new arsenal and took sleighs to Sackets Harbor. The rotting snowshoes were still on the wall when the brick building was taken down in 1850. Pike took York (Toronto) and lost his life. His body was brought back to Sackets Harbor for burial.

The second British attempt to take Sackets Harbor, on May 29, 1813, came at a time when the post was badly manned, for most of the regulars and some militia had gone with Pike. Gen. Brown rounded up 500 militia to strengthen the force of 500 regulars at the Harbor.

The Watertown Rifles, hastily organized that spring, hastened to the Harbor in full force, all except Benjamin Woodruff, who was away when the call came. He got home, heard the news, shouldered his rifle, drew powder at the arsenal, and hurried toward the Harbor. Finding that the powder was too coarse to prime his old flint-lock, he stopped at a store in the Harbor, bought powder, and joined Brown's forces.

The British landed in boats and advanced against the militia, which held out for one volley and scurried for the rear, leaving the smell of powder to the regulars. Brown, hot under the collar, rounded them up and gave them a good North Country tongue-lashing. Forming them into some semblance of order, he led them through a strip of woods in a flanking movement. The British, thinking that the militia was the regiment of regulars that was reportedly on its way to the Harbor, stayed long enough to receive one volley before returning to their boats. Thus ended the Battle of Sackets Harbor, in which both sides suffered serious losses. For his exploit, Jacob Brown was elevated to the rank of brigadier general in the United States Army.

Back at the Woodruff farm, all able-bodied men had left to fight for their country. The old patriarch of the clan, Jonah Woodruff, with the women-folk and children, climbed to the highest hill and watched the smoke rolling from the Harbor and listened to the booming of cannon and the rattle of musketry.

A surprise attack by a small British force on July 2 failed when a deserter went over to the American side, and the officer in charge decided discretion would be the better part of valor, and retreated to his boats.

The war took on a definite naval aspect. The border villages were recipients of visits from American ships and, on one occasion, a British gunboat touched at Cape Vincent, landed some of its crew, and attempted to capture three dragoons from Sackets Harbor. One of these dragoons was an excellent fencer. He held off the British sailors until his companions escaped. The British, not being able to outfence the dragoon, shot and killed him. A fortnight later, the British appeared again, plundered a store and burned some temporary barracks at Cape Vincent.

Sackets Harbor became, not only the base for Commodore

Isaac Chauncey's fleet, but a ship-building center. Henry Eckford, a genius at turning out ships in jig-time, came to Sackets Harbor early in the war. Chauncey needed a flagship, so Eckford completed the "Madison" in forty-five working days. It was not fully equipped until 1813, for everything except timber had to be brought in from the Mohawk Valley over muddy roads or run down the shore of Lake Ontario from Oswego under the watchful eyes of British ships. Eckford, by working his men seven days a week, also finished the "Pike" that same year. These workers, chiefly from the North Country, felled trees, lopped off limbs, and adzed the lumber where it fell. No time was wasted in seasoning lumber; these ships were temporary expedients to win a war. Eckford produced one warship every six weeks until Chauncey's fleet became superior to that of Sir James Lucas Yeo's British navy in number and quality of ships.

Sackets Harbor became a rowdy place. The village was unprepared for the influx of soldiers, sailors and artisans. Military discipline was severe and at times over-bearing. About a dozen military executions took place, chiefly for desertion.

Dissatisfaction with rations led to a unique demonstration. A mess of militiamen had been issued a hog's head. After morning review, they placed it upon a bier borne on the shoulders of four men. To the sound of muffled drum and a funeral march, the men paraded through the village to the cemetery, where they buried the hog's head with a solemn service.

Toward the close of the war, Eckford's workmen, whose conduct had been exemplary compared to that of the soldiers and sailors, celebrated the launching of one of his ships by getting uproariously drunk. These workmen and the sailors hated the soldiers, so three drunken artisans pounced on a dragoon, who escaped their clutches and sought protection from an armed sentinel, who fired at the drunken men and killed one of them. The ship carpenters grabbed axes and adzes and, aided by sailors with boarding pikes and cutlasses, went after the sentinel. The soldiers, in defiance, formed a hollow square around the intended victim and dared the artisans and sailors to come get him.

Brown, Eckford and Chauncey, who heard the yelling and cursing, placed themselves between the belligerent groups and persuaded the carpenters to let them take care of the sentinel. They held an examination in Watertown, and the sentinel was sent to another post far from Sackets Harbor.

Eckford turned out ships with great rapidity, but the equipment for them was often lacking. An attempt to bring armament for three ships led to the only other skirmish involving the Black River Bay area. On the evening of May 28th, 1814, nineteen boats, containing the equipment and 150 men, left Oswego for Stony Creek near Henderson Harbor. The following noon they reached Sandy Creek, but had lost one boat to the British, thus informing the enemy of what was transpiring. The boats were run up the south branch of Sandy Creek, about two miles from its mouth.

The British ships reached Sandy Creek the next day, so Lieut. Woolsey sent for the militia. At nine o'clock, a squadron of dragoons arrived, together with a company of light artillery with two six-pound cannon. The British came up the creek, landed, and were ambushed. An officer and several men were killed and the whole detachment was thrown into confusion, whereupon the militia charged from the woods with fixed bayonets and captured the entire British force.

Farmers arrived with wagons, on which all the equipment, except one large cable, was loaded. The cable was carried twenty miles, through Ellisburg and Smithville to Henderson Harbor, on the shoulders of soldiers and civilians. When the strange procession arrived at Henderson Harbor, sailors came out to meet it with cheers and led it triumphantly through the village.

The Black River valley got a thrill in September, 1814, when Gen. Izard, with 4,000 men, came along the State Road from Johnstown and through practically every village in the valley. This was the last large military group to arrive at Sackets Harbor during the war, but Madison Barracks, built in the years immediately following the peace treaty, remained a military outpost for almost a century and a half.

VI
SHIPS, COTTON AND WOOL

THE WAR lent an impetus to industrial development along the Black River and at its mouth. Gristmills and sawmills continued to flourish on the river and its tributaries, for flour and lumber were essential to feed and house the expanding population. Ship-builders remained in the harbor villages and their skills were utilized to carry on the construction of vessels for the lake trade. An embargo on English cotton and woolen goods had created a demand for these articles, so mills to produce them sprang up along the Black River.

Two of the largest vessels to be planned at Sackets Harbor were under construction at the close of the war. The "Chippewa," at Storrs Harbor, and the "New Orleans," under the supervision of Eckford at Navy Point, were to have keels 187 feet long; their beams were to be 56 feet; and each vessel was to be pierced for 110 guns. Though the Treaty of Ghent had been signed on December 14, 1814, Sackets Harbor did not get the word until March of the following year. The hulks of the "Chippewa" and the "New Orleans" had been completed, so the government had houses built over them in 1815. After a few years, the "Chippewa" was sold to an individual and burned for its iron. The famous ship-house which protected the "New Orleans" remained a landmark at the Harbor until 1882, when a strong wind blew it away. What was to have been the proud "New Orleans" was sold at auction for $400.

A tragic note was added when the ship broke in two while being dismantled; one workman was killed and two others were painfully injured. Slivers from the hulk were collected by sentimental folk, and one shrewd Watertown merchant sold canes made of wood from the "New Orleans."

The first American steamboat to operate on the Great Lakes was built at Sackets Harbor in 1816 and launched the next spring. The "Ontario," a side-wheeler, was 110 feet long, 24 feet wide, and drew eight feet of water. Her maiden trip from Sackets Harbor to Ogdensburg was greeted with bonfires along the shore. The "Ontario," designed for trips between Ogdensburg and Lewiston, puffed along at five miles an hour until 1832, when she was broken up at Oswego.

A second steamer was launched at the Harbor in 1819. She was the ill-fated "Martha Ogden," built for the firm of S. & L. Denison. She went aground in a gale at Nutting's Bay off Stony Point in November, 1832. After weathering a storm-tossed night, the crew and passengers were taken to shore in the morning, one by one, in a three-bushel basket rigged to a line with a Dutch harness.

The first schooner to reach the port of Chicago was built and launched at Sackets Harbor in 1834. The "Illinois," or "Ariadne," 80 feet long with a beam of 20 feet, sailed from the Harbor on May 12th, with Capt. Augustus Pickering, her owner, in charge. She got through the Welland Canal with difficulty and made several stops before reaching the foot of Lake Michigan a month later. Capt. Pickering found no docks at Chicago, and a sand bar forced him to land his passengers in the ship's yawl. The settlers at Chicago, pleased that Pickering had named his vessel after their state, came out and got the schooner over the bar and into the harbor.

Clayton and Cape Vincent, though located on the St. Lawrence River, have been tied closely with the Black River country. And it was these two villages which engaged in a unique operation which brought prosperity, not only to the villages, but to farmers in the North Country who had lumber to sell. Jesse Smith and Eldridge G. Merick of Clayton and Richard M. and Maj. John B. Esselstyn of Cape Vincent used quantities of timber, from the French Creek area and from the land owned by James Le Ray, for shipment down the St. Lawrence River to Montreal and Quebec. Later, they brought in staves and oak timber from the Great Lakes.

Several timber rafts, valued at $40,000 to $50,000 each, left Clayton and Cape Vincent each year. The rafts were huge affairs, constructed in 30 to 40 sections known as drams. In the early days, the rafts were equipped with sails; later, they were towed by steamboats. Each raft had a wooden cabin for the master and tents for the crew, which sometimes numbered 200 to 300 men. In order to shoot rapids along the St. Lawrence, a raft was broken up into drams, each with a pilot and men to keep the dram straight by poling. Most drams got through the rapids, but a few broke up, with the resultant loss of lumber and of men.

Winters were spent at Clayton and Cape Vincent in building steamers and sailing ships. Dr. Hough lists as having been built at Cape Vincent, between 1819 and 1853, a total of 30 vessels for the lake trade; included were 26 schooners, two brigs, one sloop and one propeller. These ships were named after such figures as Vincent Le Ray, John Marshall, Patrick Henry, Lafayette and Napoleon.

Smith & Merick, and later Merick, Fowler and Esselstyn, were building steamboats at Clayton. With one or two exceptions, all of the steamers for the Ontario & St. Lawrence Steamboat Company's lines were constructed at Clayton, also three steamers for the Ontario Navigation Company. Merick's boats were known along the lake and the river as the "Reindeer Fleet." To obtain the privileges of coasting vessels built on Canadian soil, the firm installed a shipyard on Wolfe Island. These lake steamers, after some forty years of success, lost the trade to the rising railroads. Merick signed articles of sale for his last steamer in 1886, on the morning he died.

A few vessels were launched at Henderson Harbor and

Chaumont. Builders at Three Mile Bay were turning out club boats for regattas.

Though the Chaumont Bay area possessed valuable quarries, the most exciting industry operated around Point Salubrious each November, when lake herring, known locally as ciscoes, spawned in the waters of the bay. Farmers owning land along the shore held the fishing rights, so they hired help to seine the ciscoes. It is estimated that, between 1816 and 1880, 10,000 barrels of ciscoes and white fish were shipped annually. In one boom year, so many fish were netted that coopers could not supply barrels fast enough, so the ciscoes were shipped in tanks and other containers. The industry closed about 1880. The ciscoes either had become exterminated or they had become smart and had chosen another spawning place.

Cape Vincent developed a fishing industry which did not depend upon the capriciousness of ciscoes. Brown & May from Port Ontario went into business at Cape Vincent in 1889, as did several other small firms. The industry was consolidated as the Lake Ontario Fish Company, Ltd. The company sold fresh fish, frozen fish and salted fish, and packed its product in boxes made at its own plant at Cape Vincent. At its peak, the Lake Ontario Fish Company was averaging shipments of 40,000 pounds of fish a year, and had installed a branch at Kingston, Ontario.

Brownville, in its infancy, tried to become a port. First, it attempted to get the State to improve navigation to the mouth of the Black River, but nothing was accomplished. The village next constructed a canal with locks at the rapids at Fish Island (Dexter) but, inasmuch as the locks had clearance for small boats only, the vision of a lake port faded.

Watertown could never be a lake port, for the turbulent river prevented navigation to the county seat; but that same, coffee-colored stream, tumbling a hundred feet over rocks and hurling amber-white spray toward the surrounding forest, bespoke a mighty future for the village.

Henry Coffeen, the pioneer, had shrewdly bought his land near the Great Falls. Other pioneers, forsaking the fertile soil back from the noisy river, had gathered at Watertown in the hope that the energy of the falls might be harnessed to serve industry.

A start had been made before the war. Coffeen had thrown a rude bridge over the river near the courthouse. Sawmills and gristmills went into operation near a dam below the bridge. And, with thoughts of New England in their minds, a group of citizens had donated a large plot of land in the heart of the village for a common or public square. Watertown was definitely moving ahead.

The demand for cotton and woolen goods was rising, so it seemed imperative that Watertown should have a factory in which to manufacture the much-needed articles. The year was 1813. The war was still in progress. Inflation had infested the North Country.

Nine promoters, including William Smith, the builder, John Paddock, the store-keeper, and Egbert Ten Eyck, a lawyer who had moved over from Champion after that town failed to get the county seat, organized the Black River Cotton and Woolen Manufacturing Company, with a capital of $100,000. This was a lot of money for those days, but Watertown was a wealthy village. The company encountered no difficulty in selling shares of stock.

Capt. Ezekiel Jewett owned the 400 acres extending from the center of the village to the river. He asked and got $10,-000 for his farm and $250 for a right of way from the Public Square to the factory site.

William Smith had raised the courthouse and jail and later was to plan Madison Barracks. Smith, as a matter of course, was put in charge of building the factory. A new dam was thrown across the river and a four-story structure rose at the river's edge in the summer of 1814. The cost of construction was $72,000. The factory boasted a cupola, in which hung the bell from a British frigate which had been captured by the late-lamented Gen. Zebulon Pike at York. This was the first bell in Watertown; it served to summon the workers to their jobs and may have been used to celebrate more important occasions.

The factory got away to a brave start and did well for a year or two, but the lifting of the embargo and the resultant influx of cotton and woolen goods from England brought production in Watertown to a standstill. The factory, which had cost $72,000 in 1814, was sold three years later for $7,000. Several concerns operated it until 1869, when fire left it a hollow ruin which stood until recent years as a reminder of the failure of Watertown's first manufacturing enterprise.

Jonathan Cowan, one of the group which had sponsored the ill-timed venture, owned as part of his land holdings a little island in the Black River near the Great Falls. It was judged so worthless that he offered it to Jonathan Baker for ten dollars. Baker offered five, and the deal fell through.

In March, 1827, Levi Beebee, a native of Connecticut who had settled in Cooperstown, visited the North Country in search of a factory site. He took an option on land in Brownville before he spotted Cowan's Island. He also needed the 120-acre plot in Pamelia across the river, owned by Vincent Le Ray. He let his option in Brownville lapse, thus stirring the suspicion in that village that he was to abandon them in favor of Watertown. If there was anything that Brownville hated, it was to be outdone by the county seat. A group from Brownville jumped into a wagon and hurried toward Le Rayville to buy the Pamelia land and thus block Beebee. That Connecticut Yankee was too shrewd to be stopped in this way. He and William Smith started from Watertown at three in the morning behind a fast pair of horses from Israel Symonds' hotel. They saw Le Ray and purchased the coveted land for $1,500. As they left the land office, a team of exhausted horses, pulling a wagon, arrived from Brownville. Beebee and Smith bid their Brownville rivals a cheerful "Good morning," and left for Watertown. If the crestfallen Brown-ville men made any reply, it has not been recorded.

Between spring and late fall, Smith put up a stone factory which caused gasps of astonishment in Watertown. The build-ing measured 250 by 65 feet. It had three stories and an ample basement for offices and storerooms. According to Dr. Hough: "Under the main building, two wheel pits, each 24 by 32 feet and 24 feet deep were blasted in the rock, and a canal 10 feet wide, 6 deep, and 250 long, was made, which furnished water from the smaller or south branch of the river. It was intended for 10,000 spindles, of which 3,000 were got in operation."

The factory was incorporated in 1830 as the Jefferson Cot-ton Mills, with a capital of $250,000, a sum previously un-heard of in the North Country. Inasmuch as the company planned to employ 500 workers, two massive stone boarding houses were added to the plant.

For three-odd years, Watertown's position as the manufac-turing center of the North Country was assured. The factory was doing well, and many people were gainfully employed. Watertown folks remembered for years the due bills, adorned with a cut of the factory, which could be used at stores in lieu of cash and were derisively called "Beebee's shin-plasters."

Disaster struck suddenly. On Sunday, July 7, 1833, a fire, apparently of incendiary origin, totally destroyed the factory, the dreams of Beebee and the hopes of Watertown. The loss was $200,000, only an eighth of which was covered by in-surance.

Watertown did not bury its head in the sand, though the whole community had been shaken to its foundations. Six months after the fire, the Watertown Cotton Mills Company built a mill at Factory Village. The Hamilton Woolen Mills operated from 1835 to 1841, when they went up in smoke. The Watertown Woolen Manufacturing Company and the Williams Woolen Company both established small factories at Factory Village, the latter making coarse cloth. The financial

Old Cotton Factory, Watertown. Built in 1814. Ruins from Photo by David F. Lane.

Crescent Flouring Mill, Watertown. Photo courtesy of *Watertown Daily Times*.

Mill Street Industries, Watertown, showing Knowlton Brothers Paper Mill (left) and Crescent Flouring Mill. *Watertown Daily Times*.

panic of 1837 evidently ruined both firms, for of the first little is known and the second was converted into a tannery.

Two factories along the Black River never went into operation. At Carthage, Hiram McCollum, operator of a tin shop, a nail factory and a rolling mill, built a brick factory in which he hoped to make cotton cloth, but it burned before he could use it. Down toward Brownville, James Wood's woolen mill also lost out to the elements. While Wood was waiting for machinery with which to equip his new factory, a freshet came along and swept it down the river.

Brownville, Watertown's earliest rival, entered the competition. The Brownville Manufacturing Company, with a capital of $100,000, was formed in 1814 for the purpose of manufacturing cotton and woolen cloth. A factory was built and operations commenced the next year. The lifting of the embargo evidently ruined this venture, for the factory lost money after operating but a few months. The building lay idle until 1831, when a group from Cooperstown, capital again $100,000, rejuvenated the factory and, as the Brownville Cotton Factory, carried on until 1842. The Ontario Cotton Factory took over, and employed about 90 hands to operate its 3,200 spindles and 80 looms. A small woolen factory, owned by Bradley & Brown, burned in 1846.

Fish Island, at the mouth of the Black River, gave woolen manufacture a try. The prime mover in this venture was S. N. Dexter, after whom the village was later named. The Jefferson Woolen Company factory was built in the panic year of 1837 at a cost of $140,000. It was an imposing stone building with a cupola, located on the north shore of the river below Fish Island. The expense involved in building the factory, plus a decline in the price of woolen goods, kept the company in continual hot water until it failed in 1842. The four-story mill, too good to remain unused, was sold to the Jefferson Manufacturing Company, which carried on until 1853, manufacturing 7,000 to 8,000 yards of cashmere and broadcloth per month and employing 75 hands. By 1868, it was the Ontario Woolen Mills, which gave employment to 145 people. This firm made blanketing, and produced woolen blankets at the rate of 150,000 a year. By 1887, it had long lain idle, and was purchased by Dr. Charles Campbell of New York, who transformed it into the Dexter Sulphite Pulp & Paper Company.

Sackets Harbor, proud of its new Madison Barracks, its thriving ship-building industry and its customhouse, had its sights set on greater things. It had tried unsuccessfully to get the county seat after the burning of the courthouse in Watertown. The building of cotton mills at that place and at Dexter turned the Harbor green with envy, for it boasted no stream strong enough to turn the wheels of a factory.

Three men at the Harbor came up with what they thought might be the solution to their problem. Watertown had water power to spare. Why couldn't a portion of it be diverted by canal to Sackets Harbor? The obstacle lay in the fact that the land they wanted had belonged to Henry Coffeen, whose adventurous spirit had carried him to Illinois and to his death in 1819. Son Henry H. was a chip off the old block. He owned his father's land in Watertown and would not part with it, even for the benefit of the promoters at the Harbor.

The Harbor people tried another approach. The canal would be used, not only for water power, but for boat navigation, a feature which would aid Watertown. Coffeen was not impressed by this argument. The canal promoters were forced to start their canal at Huntington's Mills, (Huntingtonville), two miles above Watertown. Undaunted, though somewhat chastened, the Jefferson County Canal Company, with Elisha Camp as its prime mover and Vincent Le Ray de Chaumont among the stock-holders, finished, in 1832, a canal from Huntington's Mills to the Harbor.

Water power turned the wheels of a gristmill, two sawmills and Camp's paper mill, but no cotton factory. The canal, known locally as "Camp's Ditch," was kept open for ten years, but the cost of maintaining the first half mile, due to flooding by the Black River, plus the burning of Camp's paper mill, led to its abandonment. Thus ended Sackets Harbor's bravest attempt to outdo Watertown.

Henderson made one stab at manufacturing. In 1814, the Henderson Woolen Manufacturing Company was organized, and considerable money was spent to get it started, but the venture never got off the ground.

Cape Vincent, Chaumont and Clayton, blessed with harbor facilities, stuck to ship-building and fishing.

VII
FRENCH LANDLORDS

WHILE the fledgling industries were enjoying success or suffering failure up and down the Black River, James Le Ray de Chaumont kept buying land until he owned the greater part of Jefferson County and large holdings in Lewis, Franklin and St. Lawrence Counties.

He had been back and forth between France and America a few times since his first voyage here in 1785, but when he returned here in 1802 his stay was cut short by the death of his father the next year, so he sailed for France to settle the family estate. While there, he reached a decision to cast his lot in the North Country, so in 1806 he sent his family physician Dr. Beaudry as his land agent with instructions to select a site and supervise the construction of a mansion in the wilderness in what is now the township of Le Ray.

The limestone mansion which stands today on the grounds of Camp Drum is not the home which Dr. Beaudry built for James Le Ray. The original mansion, which was not quite finished when Le Ray returned to occupy it in 1808, was a commodious frame dwelling. Much of the lumber that went into it came from a sawmill near the site operated by Benjamin Brown, brother of Jacob Brown.

The only existing on-the-spot description of this mansion and its surroundings came from the pen of a diarist who accompanied Gen. Brown on a visit to Le Raysville in 1819: "The seat of Mr. Le Ray is a very agreeable one," he wrote. "It occupies the summit of an eminence of considerable elevation commanding a view of Le Raysville village about a mile distant and of a portion of country exposed by means of vistas opened through and (sic) environing forests, a lawn covered with rich verdure and shaded by lofty forest trees, a sufficiency of which has been spared for security from the sunbeams, expands before the mansion house. The woods are opened in all directions by intersecting footpaths which traverse streams, ascend hillocks and plunge into little valleys affording every species of scenery for observation which can interest or delight. Every part of the estate and territory adjacent to it bears the impress of Europe."

James Le Ray tried to create a new France in the North Country. He entertained lavishly at Le Raysville. Guests arrived from miles around for dinners, dances and musicales, and hunting parties spent days in the forest. He imported merino sheep from France and raised flax for the manufacture of fine linen. He even planted mulberry trees for the manufacture of silk.

As time went on, he realized that much of his land would be sold to ordinary settlers, so he began to take an interest in the welfare of the farmer. On October 25, 1817, he became the first president of the Jefferson County Agricultural Society. The first vice president was Jacob Brown, the founder of Brownville and the hero of the Battle of Sackets Harbor. Brown was also the most important of Le Ray's early land agents, serving in that capacity until a land office was established at Le Raysville in 1808.

The chief occupation of the Le Ray family in the North Country was buying and selling land. (Dr. Hough, in his

History of Jefferson County, goes into the Le Ray land transactions in detail.) To take care of his expanding business, James Le Ray built a land office in Chaumont and put up a mansion for his son Vincent at Cape Vincent.

He returned to France in 1810 and remained abroad for six years. Vincent stayed in America and carried on the family business here. Vincent, unlike his father, was a shrewd businessman, and it was his sagacious management which brought financial success to the family.

Le Ray was living in the family château on the Loire when the Napoleonic empire collapsed, so he lost no time impressing upon the followers of the defeated emperor the possibility of re-establishing themselves in a new country. He learned that Joseph Bonaparte, brother of the deposed ruler, was in the neighboring city of Blois. He drove over to see Bonaparte and they had dinner together at the hotel.

The former king of Naples and of Spain faced a difficult situation. He would have to leave France, but he hated to lose the precious jewels and other valuables he had acquired during his brother's successful years. As the two men sat at dinner, several loaded wagons stopped beneath their window. Bonaparte told Le Ray that the vehicles contained silver, jewels and other valuables. He offered them to Le Ray in exchange for land in America and the deal was consummated. The ex-king was supposed to get 150,260 acres, located chiefly in the town of Diana in Lewis County.

Napoleon's officers also were in trouble, so Le Ray contacted Comte Pierre François Réal, who had been prefect of police during the Hundred Days, and Marshal Emmanuel de Grouchy, whom Napoleon had blamed for the loss of the Battle of Waterloo. Réal and Grouchy, together with a group of Napoleon's officers, purchased land at Cape Vincent. Réal built the Cup and Saucer House, a unique piece of architecture which he envisioned as the future home of Napoleon, for the group of officers was dedicated to rescuing its emperor and bringing him to America. It is claimed that they chartered a fast vessel but were frustrated in trying to land at St. Helena. Napoleon's death defeated the purpose of their emigration to America, so they returned to France.

The three sons of the mayor of Arras, Louis, Hyacinthe and Theophilus Peugnet, after undergoing adventures that would have put to shame the Three Musketeers, came to America and purchased land at Cape Vincent. The young men had little money, so they traded swords and pistols for oxen and plowshares, which they used to cultivate the land. The brothers prospered. Louis built a stone house outside the village, Theophilus lived in the Cup and Saucer House, and Hyacinthe purchased, from Vincent Le Ray, the Stone House which James Le Ray had built for his son at Cape Vincent. The Stone House remained in the Peugnet family until 1921. Theophilus and Hyacinthe lie buried in the St. Vincent de Paul cemetery at Cape Vincent.

James Le Ray returned to Le Raysville in 1816, bringing with him his daughter, Countess Theresa de Gonvello, and Mme. Jenika de Feriet, who claimed to have been a close friend of Mme. de Stael. Others say she was governness to Theresa and possibly James Le Ray's mistress. Be that as it may, Mme. de Feriet, who was not a married woman, came with James Le Ray and his daughter and lived in the Le Ray mansion, where her musical ability was in much demand at family musicales.

Mme. de Feriet moved out in 1820, for she had acquired land from Le Ray on the Black River at the great bend. Though historians accept the fact that she purchased this land, Noadiah Hubbard's daughter, Parnelle, who knew Mme. de Feriet well, wrote: "It is understood that she was obliged to take the land from Mr. Le Ray in exchange for a debt for a large sum of money loaned him." Anyway, she built at the great bend a limestone mansion which she called the Hermittage and she lived there in regal splendor for twenty years. Among her prized possessions were a concert harp and the first grand piano in the North Country. She rode horseback around the countryside and appeared in expensive finery at important social events in Watertown. She was truly the Grande Dame of the Black River country.

Of the French aristocrats who settled along the Black and Beaver Rivers at what was to have been Castorville, the capital city of Castorland, only a few have been mentioned by historians.

James Le Ray, on one of his trips, came to the Beaver River to find M. J. T. Devouassoux, a retired French officer, sitting in front of his cabin in morning gown and slippers. The cabin had been built on the shore of the river, where the first spring flood would carry it away.

"Haven't you some higher ground on your lot?" Le Ray asked.

"Indeed, sir, I cannot say."

"Why, haven't you explored your lands before building?"

"Indeed, no. I thought I could not possibly find a better spot than the bank of this beautiful river. I like fishing. Here I am near my field of operations."

Le Ray took the officer back from the river and pointed out a safer spot for the cabin.

A French aristocrat and his daughter had come with the first émigrés about 1798 and settled at a spot, on the Black River opposite the mouth of the Deer River, which he named Sisterfield. Louis François de Saint Michel was said to have held high office under Louis XVI, and he was remembered for his aristocratic bearing. His daughter, who had known nothing but luxury in France, pitched in like a pioneer woman and later married a local farmer. Saint Michel enjoyed visits with the Le Rays at Le Raysville and on one occasion travelled to Brownville, where he had a conversation in French with Governeur Morris, who was visiting Jacob Brown.

At the Long Falls (Carthage) Jean Baptiste Bossuot kept the "filthy tavern" noted by early visitors and also operated a ferry across the river. James Carrett, who tended the ferry, attracted the attention of James Le Ray, who took him to France. While there, the young man came under the wing of Joseph Bonaparte and returned to the Black River country with the ex-king as his secretary and land agent.

Joseph Bonaparte's connection with the North Country has received different interpretations from historians. Dr. Clarke reported that the ex-king appeared in Utica in September, 1817 while en route to Niagara Falls and in the following year made his first trip to visit James Le Ray at Le Raysville and to inspect the land he had purchased from him. In 1822, he came to Trenton Falls, where he gave money to the proprietor of the Backus Hotel to be used to blast out rock in the ravine and make a safe walk up to the first fall. Dr. Hough wrote that Bonaparte did not come to his land holdings until 1828, for he did not gain legal title to his property until 1825. Dr. Hough also maintained that the ex-king visited his lands only four times and that he merely spent summers there, but other historians thought he made annual visits.

Bonaparte built four houses in the North Country, one at Natural Bridge, a second one on the Indian River at what is now known as Anstead's Bridge, and a house and a rustic lodge at Lake Diana, now Lake Bonaparte. Dr. Clarke wrote: "these houses were lavishly furnished with works of art, tapestries, cut glass and silver." He also pictured the ex-king attired in a green velvet hunting suit and surrounded by ladies dressed in silks and satins. Dr. Hough described one occasion when Bonaparte and his followers held a picnic in the woods, "a meal which had been prepared with great care, and embraced every delicacy that the country afforded, displayed upon golden dishes, and served with regal ceremonies."

Later historians have taken the cue from these statements. The Bonaparte house at Natural Bridge has been described as a semi-fortress with bullet-proof rooms. The scow on Lake Bonaparte has evolved into a beautiful gondola, which carried beautifully-dressed ladies and gentlemen on moonlight cruises of the lake. Legends about Bonaparte's generosity are common all through the Mohawk and Black river valleys.

For approximately ten years, the Le Rays and other French settlers lived luxuriously in the North Country. Land sold readily and settlers came in by the hundreds. Money flowed in to pay for the extravagant parties.

Vincent Le Ray could see dark clouds forming to the south, where "Clinton's Ditch" was creeping toward Buffalo. He probably warned his father and the other émigrés, but they would have paid no heed. Life went on in its carefree and expensive way. With the opening of the Erie Canal, land sales fell off abruptly, for settlers preferred the rich soil of the Genesee country and the Western Reserve to the hard-won acres in the Black River valley. Some who had settled on Le Ray's land sold out and moved away.

James Le Ray went bankrupt before the canal was officially opened. On Dec. 31, 1823, he signed everything over to his son, Vincent, who strove mightily to salvage what he could of the vast Le Ray empire. He did remarkably well, though the Château de Chaumont sur Loire was lost to the family forever.

The land James Le Ray turned over to Vincent gives an idea of the size and value of the family holdings in the North Country:

Franklin County	30,758 acres	value	$ 22,500
St. Lawrence County	73,947 "	"	106,000
Jefferson County	143,500 "	"	574,000
Lewis County	100,000 "	"	133,000
Totals	348,205 "	"	$835,500

Vincent Le Ray evidently thought that the original family home was not sufficient advertisement to lure land purchasers, so he had it torn down in 1825. The present limestone mansion was started in that year and was ready for occupancy two years later. David Granger of Champion was the master builder and Roswell Murray was the master mason, according to Miss Parnelle Hubbard. Alfred Vebber was busy for months in making the doors of cherry wood paneled with the choicest maple. Everything was accomplished by the slow hand process.

The completed mansion, with its imposing Doric pillars, was at the time probably the most imposing residence west of the Hudson River. James Le Ray made his residence there until he left for France in 1832.

Joseph Bonaparte also sailed in that year, taking with him James Carrett, but leaving behind his mistress, Annette Savage, and their young daughter, Charlotte. Annette married a man named de la Folie, who squandered her money. After his death, she opened up a store in Watertown. Charlotte married Zebulon Howell Benton. The marriage did not turn out well, so Charlotte taught school in Watertown to support her and her daughter, Josephine. Tradition maintains that during the closing years of the reign of Napoleon III, Charlotte took Josephine to the French court, where Napoleon III recognized the girl as a true Bonaparte and bestowed a pension upon her. The Franco-Prussian War of 1870 unseated Napoleon III, so Charlotte returned to America. She died in poverty at Richfield Springs on Christmas Day, 1890.

The Le Rays called a halt to their activities in the North Country in 1832. They left an agent in charge of their lands and sailed for France. Though Vincent made several visits in the following years, he never made his home in the North Country again. Le Ray land was still being sold at a land office in Carthage until 1914.

Mme. Jenika de Feriet continued to live in the Hermitage, her mansion near the Black River at the great bend, for nine more years. Her land did not sell well, for it was located on the wrong side of the river. Her wealth had been dissipated by expensive living. Her friends had gone. At times, she got so lonely that she would hail a passing teamster and ride into Watertown atop a load of wood, merely to be with people.

To break the monotony, she spent a year in New Orleans with relatives. In 1841, she got her finances straightened out and sailed for France, never to return.

Joseph Bonaparte's lands were purchased for the most part by John La Farge, an adventurer who had had a fabulous career as a French officer in Santo Domingo. He bought the Bonaparte holdings in 1835 for $80,000. He was the last big French landlord in the North Country. Squatters, accustomed to the leniency of the Le Rays, learned to despise the business-like La Farge. Irate settlers at Perch Lake broke windows in his house and even took shots at him. In defiance, he built a half-house, half-fort at La Fargeville, but he did not last long there. His young wife was lonely and frightened. She convinced him that he should sell out, which he did in 1837 and moved to New York City.

The only reminders of the French landlords are a few houses that they built and the names they left on the land. Chaumont, Le Raysville, Cape Vincent, Alexandria, Plessis, Rosiere and Theresa recall the Le Ray family. La Fargeville stands as a memorial to its unpopular founder. And near the great bend in the Black River stands the bustling paper-making village of Deferiet, watched over by the ghost of the Grande Dame who settled there with great hopes and who left, heart-broken and nearly penniless.

VIII

THE BLACK RIVER CANAL

THE YANKEE SETTLERS in the North Country saw the handwriting on the wall. Something had to be done to stem the westward flow of migration along the Erie Canal and divert some of it up through the Black River valley. Otherwise, the clock would be turned back a half century, and the North Country would revert to wilderness.

Watertown had the most to lose, for it had developed the water power in the Black River and had established itself as the crossroads of the North Country. Lowville also showed deep concern, for it was the leading commercial village of Lewis County and was still casting covetous eyes on the county seat it had lost to Martinsburg.

Governor De Witt Clinton, though proud of his "Ditch," had the interests of the whole State at heart. The Erie Canal had no sooner opened when he sensed two things: the canal would need water to tide it over during the summer months; that water would have to be supplied by the Black River. He suggested to the Legislature in 1825 that a feeder be run from Punkeyville (Forestport) over to Boonville and down through the Lansingkill and the Mohawk River to the Erie Canal at Rome. He also hinted that this feeder might be developed into a canal from Rome to Boonville and possibly further north.

Settlers in the Black River country grasped at this straw. Mass meetings were held in the important villages, petitions with long lists of signers flooded the State Legislature, and newspapers kept up an incessant stream of propaganda favoring a canal. For the first time, these transplanted New Englanders put aside their petty bickerings and jealousies and united in a common front to better the welfare of the North Country as a whole.

Important citizens stood behind the canal project, including such men as Vincent Le Ray de Chaumont, James T. Watson of Watson, Isaac W. Bostwick, the land agent at Lowville, Lyman R. Lyman of Lyonsdale and John W. Martin of Martinsburg, to name but a few. The driving force behind the movement was Charles Dayan of Lowville, who had come to that village at the age of seventeen. Totally illiterate, he entered Lowville Academy as a first grade pupil and, by sheer determination, made such progress that he was soon qualified to teach school. By the time he was 27, he had studied law with Bostwick and had been admitted to practice. Dayan became a politician who served long terms in the State Legislature, where he acted as a promoter for the canal. Other legislators involved in the long fight were Francis Seger in the Senate and Gen. George D. Ruggles in the Assembly.

In 1825, the North Country still reached markets under discouraging conditions. The available roads were bad, and goods going to and from the Black River valley were high in price, due to the cost of transportation. Statistics compiled showed that Jefferson, Lewis and St. Lawrence counties were shipping 20,000 tons of produce annually, including potash, wheat, grain and flour, butter and cheese, grass seed, wool, oil of mint and whiskey. Lumber played but a small part in these estimates, but it was to become the chief item of export after the canal was built. Articles being shipped into the North Country were gypsum, bar iron and steel, dyestuffs and general merchandise. Inasmuch as exports far exceeded imports, the North Country was assured of a favorable balance of trade.

Continual agitation from 1825 to 1835 stirred the Legislature to action, though its response over these years was never more than lukewarm. Several surveys were completed, chiefly over the section to Boonville from Herkimer, Rome and Camden. A technical argument involved the type of engineering to be used, until finally the inclined plane principle was discarded in favor of locks.

The people of the North Country, convinced that the Legislature was stalling, tried private stock companies and local taxation as means for financing the much-needed canal, but both schemes failed. When Dayan tried to get an appropriation from the State to help finance the Black River Canal Company in 1828, the Senate turned down his request. In 1832, the Black River Company, with such backers as Vincent Le Ray de Chaumont, Elisha Camp of Sackets Harbor, John Brown of Brownville and Isaac W. Bostwick of Lowville, incorporated to connect the Erie Canal at Rome via the High Falls and the Black River to Carthage and Ogdensburg, Cape Vincent or Sackets Harbor. Its sole accomplishment was to build and launch the "Cornelia," the first steamboat to operate on the river.

In 1835, a proposal was made by the Legislature to enlarge the Erie Canal. To provide the needed water, a feeder was to be built from Punkeyville (Forestport) to Boonville, using the waters of the Black River and sending them down the Lansingkill and the Mohawk River to Rome.

The people of the North Country were determined not to let this opportunity elude their grasp. Representatives held a great mass meeting in Lowville on August 18th. Influential citizens attended from Rome on the south to Alexandria and Rossie on the north. Statistics were presented to prove the importance of the Black River trade and how it could be improved by a canal from Rome to Carthage. Representatives from Antwerp, Governeur and De Kalb went on record as favoring an extension of the canal to Ogdensburg.

For the second meeting, on October first, 235 canal-minded citizens gathered at Lowville, including 17 from Oneida County, 146 from Lewis County, 66 from Jefferson County and six from St. Lawrence County. A committee was appointed to draw up an address to the people of the State. This address, together with the proceedings of the two meetings, was presented as a memorial to the Legislature.

Under constant prodding from Seger and Ruggles, the Legislature passed an act authorizing the building of a canal from Rome to Carthage. A chief engineer was appointed, Timothy B. Jervis of Rome, and further surveys were ordered. Construction got under way in 1838 from Rome to the mouth of the Lansingkill. Two years later, activity had been extended toward Boonville and the High Falls, though nothing had been done about preparing the river for navigation to Carthage, and the extension to Ogdensburg had been abandoned. The North Country was to receive but half a loaf, but half a loaf was better than nothing.

The project came to a standstill in 1842. The Legislature, in that year, discovered that the State was running into debt, so it curtailed all canal-building activities. This "Stop Law" was repealed five years later, and work started anew on the canal, which was to be known as the Black River Canal. The Punkeyville feeder was finished in 1848, and Nelson J. Beach and other commissioners enjoyed the first ride on a canal boat to Boonville.

The Black River Canal was completed from Rome to the High Falls in 1855. It utilized more locks than any other canal in the world: the climb of 693 feet from the Erie Canal to Boonville employed 70 locks; the descent of 387 feet from Boonville to the High Falls took 39 locks. Limestone for the locks came chiefly from the vicinity of the canal, the quarry at Sugar River supplying the bulk of it.

The Black River from the High Falls to the Long Falls had been used by pioneers for fifty-odd years. Noadiah Hubbard had poled a boat down the river, as had the Coffeens, Jacob Brown and the first settlers at Lowville. A world-traveler, Washington Irving, made the trip in a scow during a hard shower as early as the summer of 1803. Dr. Horatio Spofford, writing in 1824, had this to say: "Should any traveler wish to explore the river, I must take the liberty to caution him not to attempt it with a drunken Indian in a bark canoe. Little is known of that part of the county (Lewis) lying east of the Black River, but that on the west where the settlements are, may be pronounced a grand tract of country . . . A canal ought to be made around the long rapids, and were this done, as it will be some time or other, the hardy sons of industry and enterprise would soon deforest the wild wastes of Watson." The canal was never built around the Long Falls, but Dr. Spofford prophesied the great lumbering operations which would soon be the support of the new canal.

The Black River had been declared a public highway from

the High Falls to the Long Falls in 1821, and $5,000 was appropriated by the Legislature at that time for improving its channel. Vincent Le Ray was interested in river navigation, for his company built the first steamer to operate on the river. The "Cornelia," 90 feet long and measuring 70 tons, started out from Carthage on Sept. 22, 1832 with a passenger list which included many prominent citizens of the North Country. All progressed well until the steamer reached a point opposite Lowville, where she ran afoul of a sand bar. Efforts to dislodge her failed and the maiden voyage ended right there. The "Cornelia" made a few trips to the High Falls, and on one occasion nearly got sucked under the cataract. Her career lasted but a year. She was dismantled at Carthage, where a freshet dislodged her from her moorings and she went over the Long Falls in pieces.

Later steamers out of Carthage had no better luck. The "William F. Lawrence," brought up from Lansingburgh in 1856, burst her boiler near the Independence River. The captain suffered severe facial injuries; a boy was blown out of a window; the engineer was tossed into the hold; and a plunge into the river saved the fireman from scalding to death. It is said that the boiler was blown to shore and that the steam chest sailed far beyond, over the tops of tall trees.

Despite this accident, the Black River Steamboat Company built, at the High Falls, the first "L. R. Lyon," and launched it on June 26th, 1856. This christening resulted in tragedy, for a platform for spectators collapsed, throwing several hundred people to the ground. One lady died a few days later from nervous shock. The "L. R. Lyon," a stern-wheeler with a wood-burning engine, was the first river boat to boast a figure-head, in this case an iron lion. She also ran into difficulty on her maiden trip down the river. At Glensdale (Glenfield) stood an old covered bridge with insufficient clearance for the new steamer. Prompt action saved the day and the trip. The bridge was torn down so that the "L. R. Lyon" could pass, and folks at Glensdale had to rely on a ferry until

Excelsior Carriage Co., Watertown, formerly the Davis Sewing Machine Co. Photo by David F. Lane.

Sewall's Island Industries. Bagley & Sewall (left) and H. H. Babcock Co. (right). *Watertown Daily Times.*

C. R. Remington Paper Mill, Glen Park. Photo from Haddock's *History of Jefferson County*.

Taggarts Paper Company, Felts Mills. Photo from Haddock's *History of Jefferson County*.

another bridge was built with a draw to accommodate river boats.

The "L. R. Lyon," equipped with wings which could be extended or withdrawn, according to the contour of the river, never would have won a beauty contest, but she, and her successor, the "L. R. Lyon II," a side-wheeler, towed canal boats up and down the river for years. They met the same fate; both steamers burned at their docks at the High Falls.

Though the new State dam at North Lake was controlling the Black River and sending water through the Punkeyville feeder to Booneville, the river from Lyons Falls to Carthage starved during the dry summer months, and haphazard dredging did not prevent sand bars from impeding traffic. Even the little "L. R. Lyon," which drew but fifteen inches of water, had difficulty making the trip to Carthage. A dam had been thrown across the river at that place in 1854, but other attempts to control the river got bogged down in red tape and tardy legislation. It wasn't until 1860 that a dam was built at Otter Creek and the Bush's Landing dam had to wait six more years.

With the river under some semblance of control, Carthage began to ship pig-iron, leather and lumber up the stream. Lumbering interests were developing from above Forestport on the Black River to Belfort on the Beaver. The total tonnage on the canal at the beginning was but 25,320; by 1866, it had reached 85,908. Lumber carried in that year totalled 29,157,124 board feet, timber 131,751 cubic feet and wood, 9,503 cords.

The canal feeder from Forestport to Boonville became a highway for picnic parties, the goal usually being Miller's Grove above Hawkinsville. Capt. Isaac Scouten's "Ollie," the smallest steamboat on the canal or river, not only monopolized trade for these picnic parties, but it also carried passengers to Boonville from Forestport and Hawkinsville. During the Presidential campaign of 1860, supporters of both Abraham Lincoln and Stephen A. Douglas held rallies in Hawkinsville and Forestport, and Boonville partisans travelled to those places in canal boats, beneath flaming torches and to the tunes of local bands.

Forty people from Martinsburg boarded the steamer "Norcross" at a landing near Lowville and enjoyed the river scenery all the way to Lyons Falls. Once there, they crossed the wooden three-way bridge to see the new Forest Church, which then stood where the Moose joins the Black, repaired to the McAlpine House for a sumptuous meal, and chugged back down the river in the "Norcross."

The "L. R. Lyon," on Independence Day in 1861, was challenged to a race by a smaller boat. The two steamers ran neck-and-neck toward a narrow channel near Carthage. A twist of the rudder sent the smaller boat against the "L. R. Lyon," which got stranded on a sand bar. The victor went on its merry way, picking up passengers that would have taken the "L. R. Lyon." The Lyons Falls steamer extricated herself from the bar early in the afternoon and continued the rivalry. As the two steamers approached the narrow channel, the smaller boat was forced toward a rocky shelf with little clearance. She had a close shave, but she made it, and probably gave the "L. R. Lyon" a toot of scorn.

Capt. George Sweet's steamboats out of Carthage did a lucrative business with picnic parties. The "F. F. Connell," until it burned at Glensdale, made many trips from Carthage to Lyons Falls. Sweet charged $1.50 for the round trip and the guests were entertained with music by the Carthage Cornet Band. In 1879, the "Nellie Sweet" chugged up the river from Lowville to celebrate Fourth of July at Lyons Falls. The feature of the day was a grand display of fireworks over the High Falls, with "rockets, tableaux fire, bengal lights, a lighted balloon, Roman candles and pinwheels. The falls were "lit up with blue, red or green, and with fire in all directions over the falls from candles, etc., making it one of the most magnificent spectacles ever witnessed in Lewis County." So says an old clipping, probably from the *Lowville Journal & Republican*.

The first canal boats to go into operation on the Black River Canal were "foreign," for they came in from such distant points as Elmira, New Hartford, Lake Champlain and the Genesee country. With the completion of the dam at Bush's Landing, shippers from the Black River country felt the need for boats of their own. Villages along the canal got into the act. Jerome V. Gue of North Western put up a dry dock and ship-building yard. He turned out few boats, but they were considered among the best on the canal. Frank Seiter and Sam Ferguson built boats "like mad" in Boonville, and Syphert & Harrig of Forestport owned a fleet of a dozen canal boats. Jesse Irons conducted a profitable boat-building business at the locks in Lyons Falls. A fleet of boats out of Carthage included the "M. M. Carter," the "A. F. Gilbert," the "S. S. Hoyt" and "Ella's Sister." Historians do not tell us who Ella was.

The big wave of boat-building came during the final twenty years of the nineteenth century, when the lumber barons, the Beaches, the Van Ambers and T. B. Basselin, constructed, not only canal boats, but steamers, to ply the river between Lyons Falls and Carthage.

IX
"KING LUMBER"

LUMBERING became big business. Virgin forests stretched for miles back from the Black River, and rushing tributaries could be utilized to float logs to sawmills. The great drives took place on the Black, the Moose, the Independence and the Beaver rivers, which drained the Adirondack forest area.

The Black River Canal played an important role in these

lumbering operations, for boats could be loaded on the canal or the Black River and for short distances up the Moose and the Beaver. Though the construction of the Black River and Utica Railroad, in the years immediately before and after the Civil War, took small goods traffic from the canal, the waterway reigned supreme for transporting lumber, and remained so until careless practices stripped the forests of available timber.

Lumbering constituted the chief activity along the canal and the river. Sawmills appeared from Woodhull Creek above Forestport to Belfort up the Beaver. Places which hadn't been dots on the map became thriving, brawling villages, not much to look at, but humming with activity. The thousands who came to these lumbering hamlets owed their livelihood to the Black River. Without it, the staggering amount of timber cut in the Adirondack forests could not have reached a market. One might safely say that, though navigation on the canal and river lasted for but a half century, the result was prosperity for the river villages. Some which rose in the shadow of a sawmill have long gone. Others, blessed with the railroad and other industries, have carried on, to look back at a short but exciting past, when lumber and the river brought them prosperity.

The pioneers felled their own trees and constructed log cabins, but before many years a need was felt for frame houses. Sawmills sprang up along the river and its tributaries, often beside gristmills to provide flour. These early sawmills served a purpose, but they played but a small part in the lumber business which was to come after the Black River Canal was opened to Lyons Falls and navigation was improved on the river from that point to Carthage.

On the upper stretches of the river, fed by Big Woodhull Creek and other Adirondack streams, and provided with an outlet over the canal feeder to Boonville, lumbering hamlets sprang up like magic. Henry Nichols and Philip Hovey put up sawmills on Big Woodhull—Nichols' mill was really on

Bear Creek, a small tributary—and began shipping board feet. Enos Crandall established himself at the fall in the Black River at what was Bellingertown and became Enos. Several small sawmills toward North Lake ran continuously.

After the Civil War, two veterans of that conflict, Alonzo Denton and Nathaniel Waterbury, opened a store at Forestport, formerly Punkeyville. The lumbering bug hit them hard; soon they were competing with Nichols, Hovey and Crandall. Another Civil War veteran, Brig. Gen. Jonathan A. Hill, a bearded gentleman who had lost an arm in the war, arrived from Maine, where he had been a tanner before serving in the Union army. With Thomas R. Proctor, a Vermonter by way of Boston, he purchased and improved a tannery on Big Woodhull, and went into business under the partnership of Proctor & Hill. Philip McGuire—called Black Phil to distinguish him from his cousin, Red Phil—gave up working in the woods at Lyonsdale and set up a mill at Forestport to manufacture spars and piles for the New York City market. The spars, made of spruce because of its straightness and lightness, were used on sailing ships; the piles, of the same wood, served in building piers along the New York water front. To complete the company, William Riley Stamburg came up from Deansboro, where he had been raising hops. He built a sawmill on Big Woodhull at Meekerville and later erected at Forestport the most imposing sawmill in the village. Stamburg claimed that water power was too slow, so he installed steam in his mill.

Forestport, from the close of the Civil War to the end of the nineteenth century, really was a port, from which canal boats left with loads of lumber, spars, hides and pulp wood—Phil McGuire had added this phase to his operations—for the Black River Canal, the Erie Canal and New York City. Like other villages devoted to lumbering and the canal, Forestport offered year-round employment for hundreds of workers. When the canal closed, late in the fall, boat-owners and their helpers took their horses into the woods to aid in skidding logs, and some of the more intrepid men participated in the hazardous drives of logs down the swollen streams in the spring. Forestport became a rip-roaring sawmill village, with six stores and an equal number of saloons catering to the constantly changing population.

Hawkinsville, on a turbulent stretch of the Black River below Forestport, boasted a large tannery and a chair factory. Eureka tannery was built by Wm. Anderson's Sons in 1852, two years after Slab City became Hawkinsville. Power was furnished by Cummings Creek, as it empties into the wildly-flowing river. The Anderson establishment consisted of a 316 by 40 foot tannery, a bark mill, a leach house and 152 vats. To house the help, the Andersons put up a boarding house and ten houses. They also operated a store, a blacksmith shop and a carpenter shop. The chair factory, operated by William Wenneis, made chair rounds and general chair stock for shipment to New York City. The Forestport feeder ran near the village, so the canal provided an outlet for these products. Hawkinsville boasted two large hotels, the Mechanics Hotel and the Union Hotel, the last of which went up in a spectacular fire a few years ago.

Port Leyden also enjoyed the prosperity brought to it by the canal and the river. Kelsey's Mills was merely a stretch of farm country with excellent water power when Gen. Ela Merriam, anticipating the arrival of the canal, bought up a considerable amount of land in 1836 and gave the phantom village the name of Port Leyden before it gained the canal. He even engaged a surveyor to lay out the village two years later.

The three big industries at Port Leyden were tanning, lumbering and an iron furnace. In the fall of 1855, Snyder Brothers purchased an old tannery and developed it into an industry which tanned 40,000 hides of sole leather a year and employed 300 men during the barking season. The tannery suffered severe damage in the flood of 1869 and burned to the ground six years later.

The lumber tycoon at Port Leyden was James Merwin,

the grandson of a man of the same name who had made his way through the wilderness to settle in Leyden in 1800. The younger Merwin had been a farmer and a store-keeper before he saw the possibilities in lumber. He put up his first sawmill on the river in 1860. Twenty years later, he was turning out 8,000,000 board feet annually.

The power in the fifty-foot fall in the river at Port Leyden lent impetus to an industry which was supposed to make the village the "Iron City." Near the close of the Civil War, a deposit of black magnetic iron ore was discovered in the gneiss rock near the river. D. H. Snyder of the tannery got interested. He and four other men formed the Port Leyden Iron Company, with a capital of $500,000. Snyder deeded 15 acres to the company and a furnace was constructed at the foot of the falls.

Harvey P. Willard, editor of the *Black River Herald* in Boonville, heard of this marvellous development, so he took time out from his war reporting to make a trip of inspection at Port Leyden. He wrote: "The Iron Age has dawned upon the denizens of Port Leyden. Their vocabulary is almost wholly made up of iron and its various classical ferrigunious derivatives and compounds. The children play with iron toys, the merchants make change with ingots of iron, their table furniture is iron, they dream of iron, their common social salutations are resonant of iron, and to such an extent does the iron mania rage, so wild their hallucinations on the subject, that it has been proposed to season their soups, salads and sauces with a pulverized mixture of the red and black *oxyds of iron*, that the men may have iron sinews, the women iron nerves, and *all* iron wills that no finite potency can successfully oppose. Should this project become practical, they will only need the art of extracting *tanglefoot* from nuggets of iron to make their little hamlet the 'hub of the universe.' "

Snyder and his associates failed, but Schuyler C. Thompson took over as the Black River Iron and Mining Company and ran the furnace until his death. A Syracuse group headed by William H. H. Gere acquired rights to the furnace in 1880 and it was put into blast in October as the Gere Iron and Mining Co. The furnace burned the following January, but was rebuilt and put back into operation in May.

Port Leyden never became the "Iron City," for the ore that had been discovered had deleterious materials in its composition. Thompson and Gere both brought in ore for their furnaces, but lack of local ore finally put an end to the furnace business at Port Leyden.

At the High Falls, renamed Lyons Falls after the Lyon family, the mother of settlements along the Black River developed lumbering and related industries. Here the river receives the stimulus of the Moose, a rambunctious stream which tumbles down through the Adirondack forest from Herkimer County. It was along the Moose that the lumber industries located. Caleb Lyon, land agent for John Greig, bought 10,000 acres of virgin forest in 1819. He settled at Lyonsdale on the Moose, threw a rude bridge and dam across the stream and built a gristmill. His son, Lyman R. Lyon, continued to buy land until he became the largest land-owner in Lewis County. Together with the Snyders of Port Leyden, he built a tannery at Moose River settlement above Lyonsdale. This establishment was operated by Henry J. Botchford of Port Leyden until his death in 1882, when it passed into the hands of Hersey & Co.

A gang sawmill stood on the bank of the Moose about a mile above its confluence with the Black. It was built by Henry S. Shedd and Marshall Shedd, Jr. in 1848, at a point where the Moose falls 45 feet. After passing through a series of owners, it was purchased, in 1874, by Lyon & Gould. The Lyon name was represented by the four daughters of Lyman R. Lyon, who had died five years earlier. G. Henry P. Gould was the son of Gordias H. Gould, a pioneer who had made a reputation as a wheelwright and builder. The father's gift to river history was the construction of a flat-bottomed boat, equipped with a stern wheel and operated by steam. He claimed that his "Excelsior," dubbed the "Beeswax," was the first steamboat on the Black River. It antedated the "L. R. Lyon," but it was built years after the "Cornelia" took to the river.

The son's contribution to the Lyons Falls sector of the Black River is immeasurable, for it was G. (yes, it was Gordias) Henry P. Gould who developed the lumber business, and later the pulp paper industry, along the Moose and the Black. Two years after the formation of the partnership of Lyon & Gould, he acquired the interests of Lyon's daughters by leasing real estate at what became Gouldtown. By 1883, Gould was using huge quantities of pine, spruce and hemlock from the Lyon forest holdings for his tannery, sawmill and pulp mill. Whereas most lumbermen were merely shipping board feet, Gould made by-products such as broom-handles, flooring, lath and wood pulp. In the last-named product, he used the slabs and edgings of spruce.

Over the long stretch of calm water from Lyons Falls to Carthage, lumbermen depended upon the tributaries for water power. Four sawmills operated on Otter Creek, run by Charles Partridge, A. C. Eaton (later Richard Carter), Edwin Pitcher and Duane Norton. The Eaton mill had a gang of 36 saws and employed many workmen. Eaton is said to have been a stingy character who would keep his woodsmen at work all winter without pay. Maybe that is why his mill burned mysteriously in 1876, destroying 300,000 feet of lumber along with it. A unique industry flourished on Otter Creek for some years, supplying butt logs of virgin spruce and shipping them to Dolgeville, where the Alfred Dolge firm used them to make sounding boards for pianos. Henry Botchford ran a tannery near the Partridge sawmill until it went up in smoke in 1870. Cyrus W. Pratt operated a tannery at Greig. His only son, Charles W. Pratt, developed a profitable lumber business out of Port Leyden, and later entered the paper-making business with G. Henry P. Gould.

The most colorful lumber baron was Theodore B. Basselin

of Croghan, who owned and operated mills at Belfort and Beaver Falls on the Beaver River, and who built, in 1885, a tremendous plant on the west bank of the Black River, part way between the mouth of the Beaver and the Castorland bridge. Basselin's mill, probably the best-equipped in the North Country, turned out 125,000 board feet a day for fourteen years and employed 250 men. Its lumberyard covered ten acres.

Also on the Black River, about three miles below New Bremen, B. Van Amber put up a sawmill and planer. After the Civil War, his sons, Watson, a veteran of the war, and Henry—both blue-eyed, black-haired and red-bearded—improved their father's plant until it rivalled that of Basselin for lumber shipments on the river. The Van Ambers were also the leading boat-builders. A settlement sprang up at Van Amberville, with the large sawmill and the shipyard serving as a core for a school, a store and houses for workers.

Independence River saw much lumbering. Henry Abbey's father had operated a sawmill at Greig, and Henry had at one time run the Partridge mill on Otter Creek. In 1885, the same year that Basselin went into full operation, Abbey built a mill back from the river (then called a creek) and carried his lumber by a tramway to the Black River. At its peak, Abbey's mill turned out six to seven million feet of lumber a year.

George Crandall, a Quaker from Massachusetts, bought an old sawmill on the Independence about a mile from Chase Lake, and developed it into a going operation, with a joiner shop, a sash and blind factory, a store, a boarding house and eight houses for workmen. This hamlet of 75 people was known as Crandallville. The mill was run by Crandall's son for eight years after the father's death in 1872.

Dannat & Pell of New York City, the largest lumber firm in the United States, had invested heavily in timberland in Lewis County. William H. Dannat, a transposed Southern planter, appeared at Crandallville one day, attired in a frock coat, striped trousers, high silk hat, gloves and cane, and smoking a cigarette. He negotiated with George Crandall, Jr. for the purchase of Crandallville.

For twenty years, Dannat threw money into the development and reaped commensurate rewards. He built a second sawmill and a factory to manufacture toys, bedsteads, tables and baby carriages. Two large dams upstream held back thousands of logs, and steam power was installed in his mills to counteract the low flow of water in summer. All the merchandise, plus the lumber, was hauled to a landing on the Black River between Otter Creek and Glenfield, where canal boats waited to transport it to New York City.

The settlement grew and prospered. A school and houses for forty families were built, the Crandall house was remodelled into a boarding house, and a post office was established. The new name—Dannatsburg. And, on an island in the river, William H. Dannat built a mansard-roofed mansion which boasted, among other luxuries, two stained glass windows imported from France.

At Croghan on the Beaver, the Rice family operated a tannery with a capacity of 30,000 sides of sole leather per year. As with all tanneries, hemlock bark was used for tanning hides. The Rice brothers purchased 10,000 acres of hemlock timber in 1870 and built a larger tannery at Jordan Falls on the Oswegatchie River. By 1883, they were conducting the largest tannery operation in the North Country. Jordan Falls, like Dannatsburg, became a village with houses, boarding houses, a school and a store.

John Felt started lumber operation at Felts Mills, below Carthage, in 1823–1824 and put up, ten years later, a big mill with four gangs of saws, a shingle machine and a planing machine. Felt got most of his timber from Pine Plains. From two to three million board feet of lumber went annually from Felt's mills, the second being seven miles up Black Creek.

Felt provided the bed-rails for the first railroad in the State, the Albany & Schenectady, in 1834. He floated pine logs down the Black River to William Huntington's sawmill at

Huntington's Mills, where they were cut into planks six or seven inches wide by two inches thick. These planks were sent down "Camp's Ditch" to Sackets Harbor and shipped to the railroad builders via Lake Ontario and the Erie Canal.

This was one of the few "wrong-way" operations on the Black River. For the most part, the trend of transportation of lumber was from Carthage, up the river to the High Falls, and then through the Black River Canal to the Erie Canal at Rome.

X

BOATS ON THE RIVER

THE RAPID GROWTH of the lumbering and tanning industries created a shortage of boats on the canal and the river. As a result, the Black River country entered into an era of boat-building that was breath-taking. Basselin and the Van Ambers put up shipyards and docks beside their lumber plants. Jesse Irons was working feverishly at Lyons Falls. Sam Ferguson and the Seiters at Boonville had more work than they could handle. The Beach brothers at Bush's Landing were equally busy. Fleets of canal boats and a few steamers to tow them along the river were constructed.

Thomas C. O'Donnell, in *Snubbing Posts*, did a great job of listing the names and owners of many canal boats which carried lumber, hides, potatoes and other products along the river and the canal. A number of these boats were built by Doran over in Durhamville; one Forestport canaller, Tom Shanks, owned a fleet of these Durham boats. Frank Seiter built about forty boats over the years. Sam Ferguson ran him a close second; his successor, Robert H. Roberts, not only built boats but served as Assemblyman and State Senator.

Roberts' untimely death while working on a boat threw all of Boonville into mourning.

Jesse Irons built some of the best boats on the canal. His craft bore family names, such as the "Frank and Lib," the "Fannie Markham," the "Lottie Corser" and the "Matt and Jess."

More boats were being built at Bush's Landing, where the Beach brothers, Andrew and Ralph, also shipped 600,000 feet or more of lumber each year. The Beach boats could be identified on the canal, for they bore such names as "Ada P. Beach," "Andrew J. Beach," "Jennie Beach," "R. Beach, Jr. & Son," etc.

O'Donnell listed many of the Van Amber boats, which usually bore family names. The "Hattie and Lizzie," known along the waterway as the "Hat and Liz," honored the daughters of Watson and Henry Van Amber.

Basselin turned out a fleet of boats at Castorland. He was not too addicted to family names, though one of his canal boats was the "Theodore B. Basselin." Two of his boats carried the names of a President and a Vice-President, the "Grover Cleveland" and the "Adlai Stevenson."

A veteran canaller, William H. Nichols, gave a reporter from the *Watertown Daily Times*, in 1932, an overall picture of transportation on the Black River Canal as it existed in the latter part of the nineteenth century. Nichols came to Carthage in 1876, when he was a lad of 14. He hired out to Nicholas Wagner and spent much of his active life travelling on canal boats between Carthage and New York.

He told the reporter that his boats carried chiefly lumber from Van Amber Brothers during the summer months. A load consisted of 75,000 feet and the Van Ambers paid at the rate of $3.50 per 1000 feet. The State charged $50 a trip for the use of canals, and steamers added $25 for towing strings of canal boats. On the last trip to New York in the autumn, Nichols would carry a load of 3,500 bushels of potatoes.

The old canaller gave a good idea of what produce the

boats carried on their return trips to Carthage. His boats came back loaded with coal, pork, salt, flour, chewing tobacco, kerosene and dry goods. It is an accepted fact that canallers hated to haul coal, and some owners returned from New York empty-handed rather than dirtying their boats with that article.

Nichols used boats built by the Van Ambers at a cost of between $1,000 to $1,300 apiece. Each boat carried three men and a cook. The average working day was 18 hours and the average distance covered per day was about 45 miles. It took Nichols three weeks to make the round trip from Carthage to New York. The earnings from such a trip amounted to about $700, on which the boat owner reaped a profit of about $350.

Horses, not mules, towed boats on the Black River Canal and at times between Lyons Falls and Carthage, though steamers usually towed strings of canal boats on the river section. Lumber was often towed as rafts.

Nichols had started working on the canal at the age of 14. George Hegeman, now of Prospect, drove horses out of Forestport when he was nine years old. He recalls the chantey he used to sing while riding ahead of the "Theodore B. Basselin."

" 'Twas in eighteen hundred and ninety two,
    When Basselin from Croghan started his crew,
'Twas jolly good fellows with him he did take,
    And safely he landed acrost Beaver Lake,
    Singing, 'Down, down, heigh derry day.'

We hired a cook, from Van Ambers' came she,
    Such a dirty old devil you never did see,
Raw beans and raw dough she would give you to eat,
    And about twice a week a big feed of salt meat,
    Singing, 'Down, down, heigh derry day.'

At four in the morning, the cook she would shout,
    'Come, boylies, come boylies, come boylies, roll out;'
We would seem not to mind her and back we would lay,

> She'd shout, 'Jaysus Croist, byes, ye goin' to
>   lay there all day
> Singin', Down, down, heigh derry day?' "

The Van Arnam brothers, Ralph S. and Lewis N., who have engaged for years in research along the Black and Beaver Rivers, stated, in *The Era of Navigation on the Black River*, that three steamboats were built at the Van Amber shipyard at Van Amberville—the "J. F. McCoy," the "Edith M. Van Amber" and "Van Amber Brothers," and that the "Nellie Sweet" and the "Oclawaha," though built elsewhere, were part of the Van Amber fleet of steamboats.

The pride of the Castorland fleet was the "T. B. Basselin," Jim Ervin, captain. Friendly rivalry existed between the steamers, and the Van Arnams tell how Ervin, in passing a Van Amber boat loading at Van Amberville, would "step out of the Basselin's wheelhouse, wave a cheery greeting to the Van Amber crowd, and shout that he would meet them at the Falls."

Serious fires aided and abetted careless forestry to bring to a close what was probably the most profitable industry ever to operate along the Black River from Forestport to Van Amberville. As we have seen, early mills on Otter Creek were destroyed by fire way back in the Seventies. Forestport had its share of conflagrations. Denton & Waterbury's first mill was burned to the ground in 1883, and Stamburg's mill, with its new-fangled steam operation, became a total loss seven years later.

Down river, the Van Ambers and Basselin were justly proud of their mills and their steamers. Together, they dominated trade along the river, but by 1899 Basselin, a man who had to be first in everything, was slowly but surely gaining control. The Van Amber brothers, at the close of that summer, decided to call it a day. They closed up the big mill and offered its machinery for sale for $1,000, though it had cost many times that sum. Basselin was the sole master. He bought up the one remaining Van Amber steamboat and added it to his fleet.

Whereas the Van Ambers carried no insurance on their property and paid little attention to fire protection, Basselin was prepared for emergencies. Ten hydrants were placed at strategic points on his property, a steam whistle was installed atop the boiler house to summon aid in case of fire, and four watchmen were assigned to patrol the yards at night.

There was one factor even the great Basselin could not control—human weakness. Everything seemed to be under control at Castorland on the night of September 19, 1899. The watchmen, after a midnight patrol, congregated for a poker game in the boiler house, and became so involved that they let the pressure in the boilers drop to a low level. When fire was discovered in the engine room, between the boiler house and the sawmill, around two o'clock in the morning, it was already out of control. The steam whistle could not blow a warning, because of the low pressure. The hydrants were of little use, for the river was so low on that September night that little water could be pumped.

It was a wild night in Castorland. With the fire raging out of control, threatening ten thousand feet of lumber in the yard, a hurry call was made for the Carthage Fire Department. When the firemen arrived, on a special train carrying a steam fire engine and hose, the mill had been consumed and the fire was demolishing the lumber yard. Basselin's loss, which included the 65' x 112' mill, the engine house, three trestles leading to the river, and the lumber yard, was estimated at $250,000.

Basselin refused to quit. He rented the Van Amber mill and operated there while his new plant was under construction. By the following spring, he was back in business at Castorland.

In late June, 1900, one of his steamers came up the river under full steam, towing a string of canal boats. The fireman

Industry at Brownville, as it was in 1890. Courtesy Gen. Jacob Brown
Museum, Brownville.

Dexter Sulphite Pulp and Paper Co., formerly the Jefferson Woolen
Company. *Watertown Daily Times.*

New York Air Brake Co. on Beebee's Island, Watertown, about 1900. *Watertown Daily Times.*

may have been striving for more power, for he had removed the spark-catcher from the smoke-stack. When the puffing steamer came abreast of Van Amberville, sparks from the stack were blown to shore, and the abandoned Van Amber mill caught fire. A bucket-brigade fought the fire unsuccessfully and the big 40′ x 100′ mill, with its saws, planer and boiler house, was burned to the ground.

Though the dreams of the Van Amber brothers had come to a close, Theodore B. Basselin's star continued to rise. His new mill was the finest sawmill in the North Country. His stately residence on the main street of Croghan, with its statue-strewn lawns, had few equals, and his stable of trotters and pacers scored successfully at fairs. His liveried coachman and his Japanese valet added glamor to the summer season at Alexandria Bay. Being a devout Roman Catholic, he contributed to St. Stephen's Church and to the Franciscan seminary in Croghan which trained young men for the priesthood. Seeing a future in "white coal," he bought up the power sites along the Beaver River. He took a definite part in organizing the Lowville and Beaver River Railroad in 1904, and became a member of its first board of directors. Everything he touched seemed to turn into gold and he became the first self-made millionaire in his section of the country.

His big mill had been shut down on Saturday evening, June 19th, 1909, for the Sunday holiday. Precautions had been taken against fire by spraying water into the stacks, but a solitary spark escaped and ignited a pile of waste slashing along the trestle which led to the river. Winds fanned it into flame and, by nine o'clock, the mill was doomed.

Ralph N. Van Arnam remembers how, as a small boy, he saw Basselin's automobile roar into Castorland over the dirt road from Croghan. Volunteers were fighting desperately to save the machinery, the boiler house and piles of lumber. Basselin could merely stand by and watch the destruction. To add insult to injury, his beloved "T. B. Basselin" had not been cut loose from its mooring at the dock. Fire caught the steamer and wind drove it out into the river, where it burned. When the boiler tipped over, a great cloud of steam rose above the water as the steamer sank.

Basselin collected his insurance, sold to the St. Regis Paper Company all of his cut logs and his standing timber, and to J. P. Lewis three power sites on the Beaver River and retired.

Capt. George Sweet controlled boating out of Carthage for many years. Together with Nicholas Wagoner and Christopher Rhiner, he incorporated, in 1858, the Carthage, Lowville and New York line, which ran six canal boats and had an office and dock at the corner of Canal and Water streets. The "L. R. Lyon" towed the fleet for two years, until 1860, when Sweet launched the "R. Gallagher." To meet the Black River & Utica Railroad at Lyons Falls, Sweet floated, in 1864, a newer and better steamboat, the "F. G. Connell," and followed it, four years later, with the "John L. Norton." Sweet did a good business, but ran into disaster in 1869, when the "F. G. Connell" burned near Glenfield, and again in 1873, when ice in the river heavily damaged the "R. Gallagher." The extension of the railroad to Carthage and the rebuilding of the Illingworth Bridge without a draw in 1902, ended practical navigation on the Black River. Sweet confined his activity to an excursion steamer, the "Outterson," which carried picnic parties about four miles up the river from Carthage to Cold Spring Park.

The great years of the lumbering industry along the Black River and its tributaries had come to a close with the destruction of Basselin's mill. Bellingertown, Meekerville, Bush's Landing, Dannatsburg, Castorland (at the Basselin location), and Van Amberville linger only in the memories of old-timers who like to recall the flourishing sawmills which once operated at those places. And the Black River Canal, which carried boats loaded with lumber up the river and through the 109 locks to the Erie Canal at Rome, has been abandoned for forty-odd years, though remnants of its carefully-chiselled limestone locks remind a tourist of its heyday.

XI
"FOREVER WILD"

Two FACTORS rose toward the close of the nineteenth century to put an end to the major lumbering phase of Black River history; the careless and wanton exploitation of the virgin forest and the creation of the Adirondack Preserve.

Loggers operated during the profitable years under the frontier "Legend of Inexhaustibility." The virgin forest from the Black River to the Adirondacks contained hundreds of thousands of acres of fully-grown trees, and the supply seemed too vast ever to become exhausted. Alfred L. Donaldson, in his *History of the Adirondacks*, wrote: "The march of the lumbermen was like that of an invading army—they attacked and destroyed the outposts first, and only gradually slashed into the inner citadel. They did damage, because they lumbered carelessly, with no concern for the future. Their worst sin was the fire menace that they left behind, and which caused incalculable destruction. Their damage to the superficial appearance of the woods, however, was negligible. Only the largest conifers were felled in the early days. All other trees were left standing. As a consequence, the spring foliage would often completely camouflage the traces of a winter's cut."

Most of the trees felled in the Black River country were white pine, balsam, spruce and hemlock. Pine was used in the building trades, spruce for spars and piles and later, along with balsam, for wood pulp, and hemlock bark for tanning.

No trained foresters cruised the woods to survey plots, estimate stands of timber and measure diameters of trees. The owner of a lumber company or his foremen merely picked out the full-grown conifers and turned the crew loose on them. Why be scientific when the forests teemed with available timber?

Winter was the season for cutting and hauling trees to the skidways to await the spring freshets. The forests to the east of the Black River suffered an annual invasion of hardy woodsmen who lived in shacks thrown up by the companies at convenient locations in the forest and moved from place to place as the timber became exhausted. Natives were joined by St. Regis Indians and French-Canadians from across the border. Canallers brought their horses into the woods and thus secured gainful employment when ice gripped the canal and the river. Lumber camps usually were located near a stream, at a point where the ground sloped from the forest to the bank. It was down these slopes that the logs were "skidded" to the bank, piled up, measured and marked with the owner's sign.

With the coming of the first pussy-willows, drives began down the swollen streams. Into camp came the log-driver, a hardy breed of dare-devil, shod with calked shoes and armed with pike-pole and peavey. It was his job to see that the logs got down the river to the mill, and to break jams of thirteen-foot logs, piled up like jack-straws. A lesser breed, known as the "flat-foot," moved along the shore and steered recalcitrant logs into the stream.

The river drive was the outstanding event of the year in river communities devoted to logging. Many tales have been told of the exploits of the drivers, and a number of homes were saddened when one or more of these daring men met death through drowning or by being crushed between logs while breaking a jam.

It was with a touch of nostalgic sadness that one witnessed the last log drive down the Moose River in the spring of 1948, for all observers realized that a glorious era had come to an end.

In reality, the day of the colorful lumberjack had reached

its sunset years before. By 1900, much of the virgin pine, spruce and hemlock had become exhausted along the outposts of the Adirondacks. The tanneries were first to go, and justifiably so, for their methods were the most destructive to the forests. Only the bark of the hemlocks was utilized in tanning, so many ambitious tanners merely stripped the bark from trees and left the naked trunks lying in the forest to rot and to create fire hazards. Years after Proctor & Hill moved from Big Woodhull Creek to Pennsylvania, piles of tanbark could be found up the creek.

The great demand for spruce arose with the wood pulp industry, a late nineteenth century development. Smaller trees could be used, so the pulp men no longer felled, not only the fully-grown trees, but began to cut trees down to 8 inches in diameter. As a result, spruce, along with hemlock and white pine, became such scarce commodities near the river that lumbermen had to keep penetrating deeper into the Adirondacks.

While this ravaging of the Adirondack forest was in progress, forward-thinking men were seeking a halt to this destruction. The leader in the Black River country was Dr. Franklin B. Hough of Lowville—physician, botanist, mineralogist, geologist and historian. State land in the Adirondacks was being sold "for a song" to railroads for rights of way. Lumbermen thought nothing of encroaching on it to further their ends. The first commission to study the possibility of the creation of State forest preserve met in 1872 and Dr. Hough served as a member. Unlike some of his colleagues, particularly Verplanck Colvin, he did not condemn the lumber interests, but advocated the principle of "perpetuation of the forest through wise use." This theory eventually led to the establishment of the Forest Service of the United States.

Dr. Hough compiled, in statistical form, various sorts of information concerning the forests, not only of his Black River area and the State, but of the Nation. He also took time to speak at public gatherings on the duty of governments in the preservation of forests.

Though the lumber interests held the State Legislature in their hip pockets, Dr. Hough, Colvin and others kept up the fight, and, on May 15, 1885, the Forest Preserve was created by statute. It brought within its borders much of the forest land in upper Herkimer, Hamilton and Lewis counties, and prepared the way for the famous Blue Line, created in 1904. The "Forever Wild" clause of 1885 read: "The lands now or hereafter constituting the forest preserve, shall be forever kept as wild forest lands. They shall not be sold, nor shall they be leased or taken by any corporation, public or private." An unsalaried Forest Commission was formed, with Theodore B. Basselin of Croghan as one of the members, which would indicate that the lumber tycoon, starting in business at Castorland in that very year, was concerned about what was happening to the Adirondack forest. Dr. Hough, who had worked so hard for this principle, and had helped to draft the "Forever Wild" law, died, on June 11th, less than a month after it was passed.

Another interest entered the field of forest preservation, on June 21, 1890, when the Adirondack League Club was organized. The club set forth three aims: 1. the preservation and conservation of the Adirondack forest and the propagation of fish and game in the Adirondack region; 2. the establishment and promotion of an improved system of scientific forestry; 3. the maintenance of an ample preserve for the benefit of its members for the purpose of hunting, fishing, rest and recreation.

The Adirondack League Club purchased 104,000 acres in the Moose River Tract, lying in Herkimer and Hamilton counties. It later acquired other land in the neighborhood of Jock's Lake, which it renamed Honnedaga Lake, and it merged with the Bisby Club at First Bisby Lake.

The two-pronged attack by the State and the club upon

what the lumber barons had considered their exclusive preserve, caused the latter to seek a loophole in the "Forever
Wild" law. It did not take them too long to discover that,
although the forest lands owned by the State could never be
sold, nothing had been written into the law about selling,
leasing or removing trees which stood on said land. The
Legislature, prodded by the lumbering interests, passed a law,
in 1893, which gave the Forest Commission permission to sell
the right to cut trees on the Forest Preserve, particularly
spruce over twelve inches in diameter. Governor Roswell P.
Flower, who had been born in Theresa and had spent much
of his life in Watertown before becoming a financial giant in
New York City, signed the bill.

The advocates of conservation, called "forest bigots" by the
lumbering interests and a number of legislators, sprang into
action. At a Constitutional Convention, the following year, an
amendment was framed to be submitted to the voters of the
State that November. It read: "The lands of the State, now
owned or hereafter acquired, constituting the forest preserve
as fixed by law, shall be forever kept as wild forest lands.
They shall not be leased, sold, or exchanged, or be taken by
any corporation, public or private, nor shall the timber
thereon be sold, removed or destroyed." The last word was
added, at the last moment, at the suggestion of Judge William
P. Goodelle of Syracuse. *Leasing* and *selling* eliminated the
lumber interests; *exchanging* wiped out such deals as Dr. W.
Seward Webb had made a few years earlier in constructing
the Adirondack & St. Lawrence Railway; *destroying* curbed
water power interests who wished to flood sections of the
Adirondacks by building dams. The electorate ratified the
amendment by a vote of 410,697 to 327,402.

At this point, a war started which has raged until the present day. It has been brought about by different interpretations
of the "Forever Wild" clause.

Conservation groups like the Adirondack Mountain Club

and the Association for the Preservation of the Adirondacks take the position that the Forest Preserve was set aside as a natural forest and should not be altered. Advocates of planned forest management contend that fallen and rotted trees make the forests susceptible to disease and easy prey to fire. The Adirondack League Club, though committed to a policy of preservation of the forests, has not hesitated to permit managed cutting on its vast preserve, and the Gould Paper Company of Lyons Falls has lumbered scientifically in the Moose River country for years.

William Chapman White, in *Adirondack Country*, after reviewing the controversy, concluded: "Between those who would cut trees for 'management' or 'improvement' and those who would let Nature and time repair the woods, while letting them stay wild, there is no easy compromise. Those who would keep the woods forever wild realize that they are taking a gamble on Nature and know that fire and disease can in the meantime be serious.

"Those who advise a new forest policy, of an open Adirondacks and a managed woods, are also taking a serious gamble. They are gambling that their changes will not so spoil the Adirondacks as to ruin the present thriving tourist trade built on people who come only because the area is 'different.'

"So long as the forest preserve is in the constitution, safe against the vagaries and ambitions of local politicians, any change will have to be voted on by all the citizens of the state. It is their woods. It should remain so."

XII

THE GOLDEN AGE OF
PAPER-MAKING

THE INTRODUCTION of wood pulp into paper-making lent impetus to an industry which had existed in the Black River valley since 1807, though never on a large scale.

This paper-making got its start in Martinsburg. Gen. Walter Martin, the founder of the village, built a small paper mill on the creek and brought in John Clark & Co. to operate it. The mill contained an engine to grind rags into pulp. Paper was made sheet by sheet and by hand pressure. The mill ran for 25 years, turning out small quantities of writing paper at first and some wrapping and wall papers later.

The paper at Clark's mill was made entirely of rags and the supply of that article was short, so Clark inserted, in the *Black River Gazette* of Martinsburg, the following poetic appeal:

> "Sweet Ladies, pray not be offended,
>   Nor mind the jest of sneering wags;
> No harm believe us, is intended,
>   When humbly we request your Rags.
> The scraps, which you reject, unfit
>   To clothe the tenant of a hovel,
> May shine in sentiment and wit,
>   And help to make a charming novel.
> The cap exalted thoughts will raise,
>   The ruffle in description flourish,
> Whilst on the glowing work we gaze
>   The thought will love excite and nourish.
> Each beau in study will engage,
>   His fancy doubtless will be warmer,

When writing on the milk-white page,
  Which once, perhaps, adorn'd his charmer.
Though foreigners, may sneer and vapor,
  We no longer forc'd their books to buy,
Our gentle Belles will furnish paper,
  Our sighing Beau will wit supply."

Despite his flair for advertising, Clark was a failure who closed out his days using the hazel rod to indicate veins of water and points for digging wells.

Gurdon Caswell, a tailor turned paper-maker, started making paper in Watertown in a two-story frame building in which he shared occupancy with a carding machine. This was in 1808, a year after the start of the experiment at Martinsburg. Ten years later, Caswell built a mill at Factory Square and moved to the bank of the Black River at Beebee's Island in 1823.

Caswell's only machine was a rag-beater. He also owned three potash kettles, set in a brick arch, for boiling rags and preparing sizing. Pulp was made from a rude vat; paper was made on frames of screen, sheet by sheet, the water being squeezed out by a hand press. The product was hung on poles to dry. With this primitive process, Caswell could produce 150 pounds of paper a day.

Caswell built a second mill at Factory Square in 1819 and a third one in 1823 on Sewall's Island. His venture did not succeed, for his mills were plagued by fire and a lack of proper equipment; but he started an industry which would eventually make Watertown one of the important paper-making cities of the United States.

Sackets Harbor took a brief fling at paper-making in 1837. Col. Elisha Camp, the father of "Camp's Ditch," put up a paper mill which burned the next year and was not rebuilt.

While Caswell and Clark were struggling to make ends meet, the first of three inventions to revolutionize paper-making was being perfected. Back in 1799, Nicholas Louis

Robert of France had patented a horizontal machine to produce a steady flow of pulp over wire. Robert's machine was made practical in England by Henry and Sealey Fourdrinier. The first fourdrinier machine in the United States was installed in 1827 at Saugerties, New York, by Beach, Hommerken & Kearney.

Two years earlier, the Caswell mills had been purchased by two bright young men from Brattleboro, Vermont. The men were not like two peas in a pod: George Willard Knowlton was cautious and conservative; Clark Rice took risks that often kept the firm in hot water. People did not write letters often enough to keep Knowlton & Rice in business. Rice, a printer by trade, was aware that district schools were beginning to abandon slates in favor of paper, and that a shortage of text books and blank books had resulted from this change.

In 1833, Knowlton & Rice built a new mill equipped with a 36″ cylinder machine and two rag engines and began to turn out quantities of books and blank books which came into use all through the Black River country. Among them were *Webster's Spelling Book, Cobb's Series of Spellers and Readers, Pierce's Grammar* and *Ruger's Arithmetic.*

Two small paper mills were in operation on the Moose River before 1850. Joel W. Ager, located below Lyonsdale, was a New Hampshire native who ran practically a one-man business for years, though he had partners at different times. To set himself up in business, Ager had a paper-making machine shipped by railroad to Rome and by ox-cart to the Moose River, for these were the days before the canal and the railroad. Ager would run his mill until he had made enough paper to fill a cart, whereupon he would go out and peddle his product in the Black River valley. It is highly probable that he collected rags on the way back in order to make more paper. Ager's little mill ran until almost 1900, producing printing and wrapping paper and employing three or four men. Shue Brothers, located at what was known as Shuetown above Lyons Falls, also produced wrapping and manila papers. It was at the Shue Brothers mill that the first experiment was made using straw along with rags to make paper.

Dependence upon rags by the early paper mills gave rise to a unique industry in Watertown, where Goodnow, Holden & Co. went into the rag business on a large scale. The firm had 45 carts travelling out of Watertown, Syracuse and Norwood, collecting rags from farmers and villagers. The business became so profitable that the company had to erect a large building at the corner of Arsenal and Massey Streets to store and process rags.

A second invention was destined to further revolutionize paper-making in the Black River valley. In 1840, a German in Saxony, Friedrich Gottlob Keller, improvised a crude, power-driven grindstone which defiberized wood held against it without substantial chemical change. He suggested to Henry Voelter that he construct a groundwood pulp machine, which Voelter did. Albrecht Pagenstecher, a German immigrant living near Stockbridge, Mass., in 1866 bought two Keller-Voelter grinders. With them, he manufactured the first groundwood pulp in this country on March 5, 1867, and the first newsprint three days later. Pagenstecher made his pulp out of aspen or popple, but he soon exhausted his available supply. He took a trip to Saxony to ask Voelter what he could do.

"We too have run out of popple," Voelter told him, "but we are using spruce. Have you any spruce in America?"

The late A. B. Recknagel of Cornell used to tell how his uncle, Albrecht Pagenstecher, returned to this country and took a trip into the Hudson and Sacandaga river region, where he found spruce in abundance. The Hudson River Pulp and Paper Company started making groundwood pulp and newsprint out of rags and wood pulp at Palmer near Luzerne in 1869.

By this time, Illustrious Remington and his three sons, Hiram, Alfred D. and Charles R., were manufacturing a ton of newsprint daily in Juhelville, the east corner of Watertown, using four rag machines and an 84" fourdrinier machine. Alfred D. Remington saw a future in the use of wood pulp and by 1870 the Remingtons had built three mills on Sewall's Island in Watertown. These mills used the Voelter process and the content of the Remington newsprint was 75% rags and 25% wood pulp. In this way, the Remington mills were able to produce newsprint for two and a half to three cents per pound when all rag content paper cost seven to ten cents a pound to manufacture.

A third invention stirred the Remingtons to greater things. In 1867, Benjamin Tilghman, an American chemist, discovered that sulphurous acid dissolved the ligneous constituent in wood, leaving a residue of cellulose fibers. He never developed his process to practical use, but A. D. Remington learned that a Swede, Carl Daniel Ekman, was teaching papermakers in his country to make paper entirely out of wood pulp by using a sulphite process. Remington went to Sweden to observe this miracle, which so impressed him that he imported Swedish chemical fiber for several years and later developed the process in his own sulphite plant on Sewall's Island.

The Remingtons had been selling newsprint to the *New York Times*. They got an order for ten tons of newsprint, stipulating that no wood pulp be used. A. D. Remington, proud of his new product, filled the order with wood pulp newsprint and sent along a note, asking the *Times* to try it. The newspaper would have no part of this experiment. It sent word to Remington to come and get his paper, which he did. It was not long before the *Times* was willing and eager to get this new and cheaper newsprint.

The revolution in paper-making in the Black River area was complete: fourdrinier machines became bigger and bigger and faster and faster; the demand for spruce employed all the energies of the lumbermen and practically denuded the virgin forests; the unpleasant odor of the sulphite mills replaced the equally unpleasant odor of the tanneries. Other paper-makers, encouraged by the success of the Remingtons, embarked on an expensive program of mass-production of wood pulp news-print.

The "grand-daddy" of them all, Knowlton Brothers, did not climb onto this bandwagon. The original firm of Knowlton & Rice had sold out to other interests in 1854, but by 1861 two young sons of George W. Knowlton had bought the Knowlton & Rice paper mill. John Calvin was 24 years old and George W., Jr. was 22. Between them, they had $1,200 and an endorsed note from their father for $5,000. The partnership became known as Knowlton Brothers. After escaping the great flood of 1869 with minor damage, the Knowltons installed a new fourdrinier machine. Four years later, they began to manufacture colored papers under the supervision of Frank A. Fletcher, a veteran New England paper-maker who had seen that type of work being done in Holyoke, Mass. The Knowltons still believed in using rags, for their product was fine paper, but they installed two pulp grinders and made some paper that was 75% rags and 25% wood pulp. By March 12, 1892, George W. Knowlton had died and John C. Knowlton had retired from the business. Knowlton Brothers was incorporated on that date with George W. Knowlton, Jr. as president, an office he held until his death in 1931.

The only other mill designed to manufacture rag content paper went up below Watertown at Jim Wood's Falls, later Glen Park. Its founder was John T. Tilden, who had peddled rags for Goodnow, Holden & Co. and became a partner in the firm of Holden & Tilden and later the sole owner. Tilden, like the Knowltons, was a rag man. He bought the water power at Jim Wood's Falls, which had not been used since Wood's ill-fated woolen mill had been swept away by a freshet years before. The water rights cost him between $1,800 and $1,900. He threw a dam across the Black River and built what was at the time the best-designed paper mill in the North Country. The Tilden Paper Company went into operation in 1888. It had two fourdrinier machines, one of them being the first built by the new Watertown firm of Bagley & Sewall. It was an 86″ machine which operated at the rate of 300 feet a minute. This installation committed the Tilden Paper Company to mass-production of newsprint, and earlier provisions made for the manufacture of rag content paper were abandoned. The Tilden name lasted but one year. The Ontario Paper Company was incorporated, with George W. Knowlton, Jr. as president. The imposing stone mill, located on the north shore of the river, employed 70 to 80 hands and manufactured 20 tons of print paper each day to the value of $1,200.

The Remingtons began to branch out in all directions. In addition to their mills on Sewall's Island, they built the C. R. Remington and No. 4 mills at Glen Park and a big pulp and paper mill at Black River.

About 1895, when the Remington operations were at their peak, the family mills had an invested capital of $1,350,000, which included 26,000 acres of Adirondack timber land. The combined mills turned out 40 tons of wood pulp, 20 tons of chemical fiber, and from 32 to 36 tons of newsprint every day. About 200 men were employed and the value of the daily output ran from $2,300 to $2,500.

C. R. Remington also became interested in the water power at Brownville. In 1893, he and J. Munson Gamble bought the property of the abandoned Ontario Cotton Company factory on the north bank of the Black River and converted it into a paper mill known as the Brownville Paper Company. Four years later, they acquired the Globe Paper and Fiber Company plant on the south bank and built a bridge to connect the two mills. The fiber mill burned, whereupon Gamble put up a new mill known as the Brownville Board Co.

A third family joined the Knowltons and the Remingtons in 1884, when Col. James T. Outterson, a Civil War veteran, and his son, James Andrew Outterson, entered the paper-making field. "Young Jim," as the son was known, was a real "ball of fire." He started in making paper out of rags, straw and old paper in a rented mill at Brownville. In 1885, he built the stone factory on the north shore of the Black River at Brownville below the Brownville Paper Company. This mill, originally called the Outterson Paper Company, was later familiar to Brownville people as the Harmon Paper Company.

Jim Outterson foresaw the coming use of wood pulp in paper-making. He journeyed to Alpena, Michigan and purchased a supply of wood pulp at a cost of $100 per ton delivered at Brownville. He developed a pulp-grinding method known as the Outterson process and claimed that he was the first man in the Black River valley to produce paper made entirely from wood pulp.

The Outtersons could not stay in one place. We next find them on the Moose River, where they put up the mill which was to become Moyer & Pratt and also the Fond du Lac Paper Company mill at Fowlerville. They may have built the latter company's mill at Port Leyden. "Young Jim's" most spectacular feat took place in 1894, when he ventured six miles into the wilderness to build a paper mill on the Oswegatchie River at Newton Falls.

His next stop was Carthage, a village with good water power which had dabbled in iron furnaces, milling, tanning and wood products, but had not engaged in paper-making. "Young Jim" conducted a one-man revolution in Carthage. Within the space of eight years (1897–1905), he built or was instrumental in building five paper mills and a sulphite mill.

Outterson was a gambler. He would announce that he would get a new mill into operation at a certain date and would place bets with villagers. He had lost sundry suits, cigars, etc. by missing out by a short space at Newton Falls. Carthaginians were aware of that fact, so he got plenty of bets in that village when he announced that the Carthage Tissue Paper Mills Company plant would go into operation on or before May 1, 1897. He collected them, for he beat the deadline by several days. The mill proved to be too small to take

Low Water on the Moose River at Gouldtown. Fynmore Photo.

High Falls in Flood at Lyons Falls. These two photographs show the capriciousness of the Black River and its tributaries. Fynmore Photo.

The Black River at Port Leyden. School is occupying site of Snyder Bros. tannery. Fynmore Photo.

The Black River at Lyons Falls, showing the Gould Paper Company and the Three Way Bridge. Fynmore Photo.

care of the orders that poured in. Outterson took this all in stride. He built another mill around the first structure and, when it was completed, he tore the first mill down.

His venture with the West End Paper Company ran into difficulties. This mill, built on property formerly occupied by Dr. Franklin Evans Robinson's pulp and casket mill, was put up too hurriedly and had to be rebuilt. Floods and ice jams damaged it over the ensuing years.

Three other mills had no trouble, the Carthage Sulphite and Pulp Company (1898), the Champion Paper Company (1902), and the Le Ray Paper Company (1904). These three brick mills were consolidated as the Carthage Sulphite and Paper Company in 1911.

Maxwell, Yousey & Company built a groundwood pulp mill on Tannery Island in 1896 and added a paper mill in the following year. The Island Paper Company made manila paper with two machines, one of them being purchased from Black & Clawson of Hamilton, Ohio. The mill was sold to Charles W. Pratt of Boonville in 1901.

Jim Outterson retained his interest in the mills at Newton Falls and Carthage, but he sold the Outterson Paper Company in Brownville to John J. Warren, a veteran paper-maker who had held responsible positions with the Remingtons and with the Ontario Paper Company. Warren also bought the St. Lawrence Paper Company, which had been built at Dexter in 1889 and had been turning out eight tons of pulp and 10 to 12 tons of print each day. Warren converted this mill to the manufacture of grease-proof parchment under the name of the Warren Parchment Company.

The Frontenac Paper Company at Dexter started up in March, 1890, with three pulp grinders and a Bagley & Sewall fourdrinier machine. This firm turned out about eight tons of print per day and employed about 30 men. Its Rex grade of wrapping paper was the strongest made in the United States.

The third mill at Dexter, the Dexter Sulphite and Paper

Company, got its start when E. F. Bermingham and Dr. Charles E. Campbell of New York took possession of the abandoned Jefferson Woolen Company plant. Dr. Campbell consulted Jim Outterson, and the mill was converted in 1887 into a factory which made wood pulp from the Mitscherlick process, a slower operation which made stronger fiber, which commanded a higher price. The daily output of this mill was 20 to 25 tons of fiber per day, and its product was shipped to paper mills to take the place of rags in the manufacture of newsprint and cheap manila paper. About 1908, a bag factory was added which produced about 4,000,000 bags daily until 1938.

While the Remingtons, the Outtersons, the Warrens and the Campbells were engaging in mass-production of newsprint and coarse papers, a unique paper-making industry was flourishing on the north shore of the Black River at Pamelia, within the corporate limits of the city of Watertown. Byron B. Taggart, a farm boy from Le Ray, had taught school and had tried a fling in the West before settling in Watertown in 1856. The flouring mills needed containers for their product and cotton sacks were expensive. Taggart, in a little plant on Beebee's Island, began to experiment with the manufacture of paper bags. His work was interrupted by the Civil War, in which he served as a captain. He returned to Watertown and developed a good business in paper bags, but he had to buy paper. In 1886, he purchased the Angel distillery at Pamelia and started making paper bags under the firm name of Taggart Brothers' Paper & Bag Company.

The Taggarts owned the best water power on the Black River and their machines were driven by that power. The chief product of the mill was bags for flour. Wood pulp was too brittle, so the Taggarts used old rope, manila or hemp in making these bags. They also developed a process whereby they could produce bags with colored coating on the inside in sharp contrast to the white exteriors, which were printed at the mill. The Taggarts turned out 25,000 fifty-pound sacks a day.

They moved into the production of coarse paper in 1889. An old factory at Felts Mills had burned, so B. B. Taggart, together with W. W. Taggart, David M. Anderson and George C. Sherman of Watertown, bought the water rights at that place, rebuilt the dam and put up the Taggarts Paper Company mill, which manufactured pulp paper, newsprint, poster paper and telephone books. One of its ventures was the manufacture of newsprint for the *Pittsburgh Press*.

The Taggarts Paper Company also purchased the Lefebvre pulp mill, located midway between Felts Mills and Great Bend. Raw pulp was sent down to the Taggart plant at Felts Mills through a piping system which led directly to the paper-making machines.

The incorporation of the Taggarts Paper Company introduced a new phase into the paper-making picture in the Black River valley. The early companies had been chiefly family affairs, and the owners had been paper-makers. Sherman and Anderson, on the other hand, had little knowledge of the technical side of paper-making. They were capitalists who saw a future in the mass-production of newsprint and were willing to invest their money in the industry. In addition to their interest in the Taggarts Paper Company, which became the Sherman Paper Company, they purchased, from Frank A. Fletcher, the Great-Bend Paper Company. This mill had been built by George Clark in 1869 to manufacture strawboard. Wall paper was made here until 1914, when the mill was converted to newsprint.

By 1900, the Remingtons had passed out of the paper-making picture, as far as the Black River was concerned. The big International Paper Company, which had purchased the Ontario Paper Company mill at Glen Park in 1898, bought the Remington mills on Sewall's Island and at Glen Park the following year.

Upriver, on the Moose and the Beaver, two paper-making

companies were getting under way which would, in time, outstrip most of their predecessors.

G. H. P. Gould, the lumber baron, had purchased the water power at Lyons Falls. The Fond du Lac Paper Company was operating two small, one-machine mills at Port Leyden on the Black and at Fowlerville on the Moose, the latter a mill that had been built by Col. James T. Outterson. When the Fond du Lac Paper Company went into the hands of a receiver in 1892, Gould attended the sale in the hope of purchasing the property cheap. Here he encountered Charles H. Pratt, another lumber baron who was later to acquire the Island Paper Company in Carthage. The bidding began. Gould and Pratt became the chief bidders. After the price had begun to rise, the two lumber barons went into a huddle and decided to pool their resources instead of bidding against each other. They got the two mills. The Fowlerville mill burned, but the mill at Port Leyden was operated by the Goulds for many years.

In 1894, Gould built, at Lyons Falls, a mill equipped with two fourdrinier machines and later added a third machine. To consolidate his interests, he purchased the International Paper Company's mill at Kosterville on the Moose in 1906. This mill, which made pulp for shipment to paper mills, had been managed for years by Maj. John S. Koster, a Civil War veteran who wore an artificial limb, for he had lost an arm at the Battle of Cold Harbor.

At Lyonsdale on the Moose, William Moyer and Charles H. Pratt, operating as Moyer & Pratt, Inc. in the mill built by Jim Outterson, installed one of the largest fourdrinier machines built by Bagley & Sewall, and made wrapping paper and toilet paper.

Lewis and LeFever are the names closely associated with pioneer paper-making on the Beaver River. Back in 1882, James P. Lewis, Charles Nuffer and Martin R. LeFever started to manufacture wood pulp for paper in a small plant at Belfort. Seven years later, Lewis, Slocum and LeFever put up a one-machine wooden paper mill at Beaver Falls. It burned in 1898 and was rebuilt. This mill is now being used by the Latex Fiber Industries. At one time, Lewis, Slocum and Le-Fever also ran a pulp mill directly across the river, and connected it to the paper mill by a wooden trestle. Lewis and Nuffer built what is now the No. 1 mill of the J. P. Lewis Co. The partnership was dissolved and Lewis put up the No. 2 and No. 3 mills. The mill occupied by Beaverite Products, Inc. was built about 30 years ago by Howard LeFever, father of DeWitt LeFever of Beaverite. The mill originally turned out gaskets and was not particularly successful until the son took over the management.

By 1900, a shortage of spruce pulp wood was beginning to pinch mass-production of newsprint along the Black River and its tributaries. The many mills, with their big, fast four-drinier machines, had an appetite for wood pulp which was rapidly exhausting the supply of that article. The Adirondack Preserve, the lumbering ground of the Basselins and the Van Ambers, had been cut off by the constitutional amendments of 1885 and 1894. The low stages of the Black River in summer also hampered the paper-makers by adding to the expense of production, for steam had to be used to run the machines and coal, transported from great distances over the railroads, rose in price year by year.

As a result, the last big mill to be erected on the Black River between Carthage and Dexter was the St. Regis Paper Company plant at Deferiet. The prime movers in this venture were George C. Sherman and David M. Anderson of the Sherman Paper Company, with mills at Felts Mills and Great Bend. The best water power between Carthage and Deferiet was at Herrings, but it was owned by William P. Herring and his son, Fred M. Herring, who were using it to operate a mill at Herrings. The next best choice was a mile and a half down the river, but C. H. Remington had purchased the water power at that point, where he planned to build a mill, but lacked the necessary financial backing. After considerable hesitation, he sold his water rights to Sherman and Anderson. The Black River starts its great bend near that point, so the St. Regis people decided to carry water from their dam to their mill via a canal. Here they ran into financial and technical difficulties and had to call on the Knowltons for assistance. The canal, a considerable engineering feat for its time, was built under the guidance of Theodore E. Knowlton. The mill, designed for mass production, had three fourdrinier machines measuring 145", 126" and 110", respectively, for the manufacture of newsprint. A smaller 90" machine was installed to make bag paper. The mill went into operation in 1901.

The Sherman Paper Company and the St. Regis Paper Company now controlled water rights and mills from Carthage to Watertown with the exception of the pulp and paper mill at Herrings and the Jefferson County Paper Company at Black River. These mills were owned by the Herrings, father and son, who had also operated the St. Lawrence Paper Company at Dexter before selling it to John Warren. Fred W. Herring died in 1912 and his father, in poor health, sold the mills at Herrings and Black River to the St. Regis Paper Company.

By that time, Sherman and Anderson had sold out their interests in St. Regis to G. H. P. Gould, so the Goulds and the Knowltons owned the company. The growing settlement at the St. Regis mill had been named Eggleston after the company's first president, George Eggleston Dodge, but its name was changed to Deferiet in 1901, a year after George W. Knowlton assumed the presidency.

During the regime of the Knowltons and the Goulds, large newspapers, in desperate need of newsprint, were seeking to buy paper mills to produce the needed product. The Remingtons, after selling out to International Paper Company, had started anew at Norfolk and Raymondville on the Raquette River. The Remington Paper and Power Company, with a capacity to turn out 175 tons of newsprint daily, overtaxed the financial resources of the family and the company filed a petition of bankruptcy in 1914. The Pulitzer and Hanna interests competed for the purchase of the plant. Mark S. Wilder bought the mills after strenuous competition with the Pulitzers. He sold them in 1916 to the Hannas, owners of the Cleveland newspapers.

St. Regis fought a battle with another newspaper, *The New York World*, in that same year. St. Regis had been tied up for several months in 1915 by a serious strike which became so riotous that the National Guard from Watertown had to be sent to Deferiet to maintain order. *The World*, part of the Pulitzer chain which had failed to get the Remington mills on the Raquette River, offered to buy St. Regis. G. H. P. Gould went to New York to talk things over and was on the point of selling when the representatives of *The World* asked for 36 hours "to consider the proposition."

Gould was no man for delay. "I will not give you 36 seconds," he snapped. "It's now or never." *The World* could not make up its mind, so Gould packed his bags and left New York.

The old-line paper-makers stepped out and the capitalists stepped in when the St. Regis Paper Company was sold by Gould and Knowlton in 1916 to a Watertown group which included David M. Anderson and Floyd L. Carlisle, the president of the Northern New York Trust Company.

The new owners had ample capital, so they threw it into improvements at all three plants. Machines were rebuilt and speeded up, and a big groundwood pulp mill was put up at Deferiet. Though they had inherited 58,000 acres of timber land, they purchased 24,500 acres of Adirondack timber and 177,500 acres of Canadian wood lands. Deferiet became a company-owned village. By 1922, it had a population of about 1,500, living mostly in company-owned houses and being entertained by a multiplicity of recreational features.

With the building of the village of Deferiet, mass-production of wood pulp and paper reached its high-water mark along the Black River and its tributaries. Thirty-two pulp and paper mills and six pulp mills were using the water power of the Black, Moose and Beaver rivers. Production was at its highest peak and over two thousand workers gained employment in the many mills. The Black River area became noted for paper-making, and Watertown was recognized as the paper-making capital of the State.

XIII
WATERTOWN DEVELOPS HEAVY INDUSTRY

GEORGE GOULDING arrived in Watertown in the spring of 1823, established himself in a small machine shop on Sewall's Island, and began to install all kinds of machinery in the mills. Goulding, a mechanical genius, was also an unselfish teacher. Among his apprentices were Theodore Woodruff, who first conceived the idea for a railroad sleeping car; Gilbert Bradford, who, with the help of Moses Eames, built the first portable steam engine; and William E. Everett, who was sent to England by the United States government in 1857 to assist in laying the Atlantic Cable.

A leading industry in Watertown before and after the Civil War was flour-milling. Joseph Sheldon and Philo C. Moulton pioneered this industry, which was concentrated near the water power at Beebee's Island. In 1835, they built the Union Mill, probably the largest flouring mill in Watertown, on the south bank of the river; a year later, they put up, at the corner of Mill and Moulton streets, the Cataract Flouring Mill. Moulton was also instrumental in erecting the Excelsior Flouring Mill on nearby River Street in 1845; this mill later became A. H. Herrick & Son. Other flouring mills in Watertown were the Jefferson Mills, which adjoined the Union

Mill, the City Flouring Mill on Newell Street, which was swept away by a flood in April, 1896, and the Crescent Mills, located near the Knowlton Brothers paper mill. The Crescent Mills, owned and operated by Farwell & Rhines, produced 100 barrels of flour per day. Some of its brands might bring a touch of nostalgia to older people—"Atlantic," "Farwell's Best," "North Star," "Pansy" and "Superlative."

Two Watertown lawyers, George A. Bagley and Edmund Q. Sewall, gave up their practices to join forces with George Goulding. To supply the needs of the flouring mills, Goulding, Bagley & Sewall made chiefly flour mill machinery, plus special tools designed by Goulding. They also acted as trouble-shooters for these mills. Bagley & Sewall became sole proprietors in 1860, though Goulding stayed on as superintendant for five years.

When wood pulp began to replace rags as content for paper, Bagley & Sewall made, for a Herkimer paper company, what may have been the first Voelter grinder manufactured in the United States. They also built the first spring wet machine to handle pulp made from the grinder. In 1889, they erected new buildings on Sewall's Island and installed machinery for the manufacture of paper-making machines, both cylinder and fourdrinier. Their first fourdrinier machine was installed in the Ontario Paper Company's plant at Glen Park.

Gilbert Bradford, a Goulding pupil, entered into business with Charles Brooks Hoard to form the Portable Steam Engine Company in 1849. This firm made portable steam engines for printing presses. Hoard, who was Democratic representative in Congress from 1857 to 1861, contracted to make rifles for use in the Civil War, but he got into a "hassle" with Secretary of War Edwin M. Stanton and his rifles were rejected. Hoard lost his fortune and left Watertown. The steam engine company was rescued by John C. Knowlton and other Watertown businessmen and went back into business as the Watertown Steam Engine Company, with a new plant. This company, the first heavy industry in Watertown, gave work to 100 people at a time when Bagley & Sewall were employing half that number.

A new industry arrived in Watertown in 1868 when Job Davis, inventor of the sewing machine of that name, talked John and Joseph Sheldon into raising capital amounting to $150,000. Business started in an old building on Beebee's Island. Sales sky-rocketed, so the Sheldons had Norris Winslow put up a new factory on Sewall's Island. By 1875, the Davis Sewing Machine Company was employing 175 men. The company band was so popular that it was chosen to greet President U. S. Grant with martial music on his visit to Watertown in 1872. The bubble burst in the late 1880's, when claims of poor workmanship, failure to pay dividends to stockholders, and an expensive law suit caused the Davis Sewing Machine Company to move to Dayton, Ohio, where it operated until 1924.

One of the Davis employees was Joseph Wise, an expert mechanic. He left Davis and branched out on his own, making sewing machine hardware, much of which he sold to the Davis people. He took his son into partnership. After the father's death in 1886, James B. Wise bought out the other heirs and developed a lucrative business in the manufacture of hardware specialties, locks, hinges and bell-pulls.

Another mechanical firm opened up on Beebee's Island in 1891. The Harmon Machine Company, in which the Knowltons had an interest, did a general machine shop business and some forging and hydraulic work. This firm took care of most of the mill repairs along the river and employed from 30 to 50 skilled mechanics at different times.

At Carthage, the Wendler Machine Company was fulfilling a similar need for that village. This firm was located in the old Empire Steam Company plant on West End Avenue. The Wendlers enlarged their machine shop and built a large foundry, later adding a brass and bronze foundry. Alexander Wendler, a native of Germany, had worked in the best paper mills and machine shops in that country. At Carthage, he supervised the manufacture and installation of machinery for pulp and paper mills.

Col. William Lord, who had made the first iron plow in the North Country for Moses Eames of Rutland, built a factory on the Black River at Brownville, where he manufactured, not only iron plows, but cast-iron stoves. His brother Judah moved to Watertown and established a foundry on Beebee's Island. The colonel's son Gilderoy joined Judah in the manufacture of plows and carpenters' tools. Judah made improvements in plows and invented the Young Mowing Machine. The factory, located across the narrow north channel from Knowlton Brothers, was wiped out in the flood of 1869 and had to be rebuilt. Gilderoy Lord, as mayor of Watertown, met Gen. Grant's party in Carthage and escorted it to the Woodruff House in 1872.

Carriage-making had gone on in Watertown and other villages for years, but it was not until H. H. Babcock entered the field that the industry played an important part in the life of Watertown. Babcock had been in business for a long time, first as a maker of wooden pumps and later as a manufacturer of flouring mill machinery. In 1880, he started making parts for carriages. Two years later, he formed the H. H. Babcock Company, which included four Babcocks and two Flowers, one of whom was to become Gov. Roswell P. Flower. The Babcock company, at its peak, around 1900, owned, along the river near Sewall's Island, buildings with floor space covering ten acres. The firm employed 350 hands.

The Watertown Spring Wagon Co., which antedated the Babcock firm by five years, was organized by Norris W. Winslow, the chief builder in Watertown at that time. Winslow put up a four story factory on Factory Square and began to manufacture platform wagons. For about 25 years, the Watertown Spring Wagon Co. produced 4,000 vehicles a year, including phaetons, cabriolets, surreys and open road wagons. Winslow had also built the Davis Sewing Machine plant on Sewall's Island. In 1889, after the Davis people had moved to Ohio, the factory was purchased by the Excelsior Carriage Company, whose president was George B. Massey, a grandson of Hart Massey. Excelsior employed 100 men in turning out a complete line of buggies, surreys and wagons. The Union Carriage & Gear Company, in which James B. Wise was a prime mover, along with William W. Conde and W. O. Ball, erected a four story factory on Newell Street in 1888 in which carriages, cutters and carriage gears were manufactured.

The four big carriage-making concerns, in 1900, were turning out thousands of vehicles and were employing 700 men. The *Watertown Daily Times,* in commenting on a record-breaking season, reported: "It is not evident, from the present status of the industry, that the passing of the horse is in any way imminent."

Even the *Times* could be wrong. When the first Stanley steamer and Locomobile chugged into the city, the carriage industry treated these invaders with scorn. It roared with mirth when a race between a horse and an automobile at the Governeur Fair resulted in an equine victory. Laughter turned to dismay as more and more citizens abandoned horses and carriages to endanger their lives in snorting automobiles.

The H. H. Babcock Company saw the handwriting on the wall. In 1909, the firm purchased the Watertown Spring Wagon Company plant and announced that it would add automobiles to its line. The Babcocks made a few good automobiles over the next four years, though they imported the engines and concentrated on expert body-building. Their product proved too expensive to compete with automobiles turned out elsewhere, so the company abandoned the manufacture of automobiles and concentrated on producing bodies for Franklin, Lincoln and other firms. World War I found the Babcock Company engaged in building ambulance bodies.

The Union Carriage & Gear was either unwilling or unable

to adjust its plant to new conditions and the factory was closed in 1916. The Excelsior Carriage Company made a desperate effort to remain in business, for it was employing 85 men. Excelsior turned from carriages to baskets, crates, shock absorbers; in fact, anything to stay in business. Its efforts were to no avail. Excelsior closed its doors in 1920. Six years later, the proud H. H. Babcock Company was declared insolvent. The carriage industry, once the pride of Watertown, had gone the way of flour milling, sewing machines, and portable steam engines.

Today's "bread and butter" industry in Watertown had its start back in 1861, when Lovett and Moses Eames, farmers and cheese-makers from Rutland, bought Beebee's Island and started a machine shop by remodelling some of the buildings which had survived the cotton mill fire of 1833.

Fred M. Eames, nephew of Moses Eames, was an erratic genius who had been working for some time trying to develop a vacuum brake for railroad cars. On Feb. 14, 1876, he incorporated the Eames Vacuum Brake Company and began to manufacturing his product at the Eames shop on Beebee's Island. Eames sailed for England, taking with him a Baldwin locomotive equipped with his vacuum brake. A test run on the Great Northern Road proved successful, but Eames discovered that, during his absence from America, a New York firm which had a claim of $47,000 against his company had taken over operation of the Watertown plant. Eames returned to this country and sued the New Yorkers. The Court ruled that he owed the money but the plant was to be returned to him.

Eames came to Watertown to reclaim his property. He was denied admission by Charles Higman, who was unaware of the Court's decision. A wild argument ensued. Higman retreated into the pattern room and locked the door. Eames, not to be halted by such a maneuver, put a shoulder to the door and broke it in. Higman drew a revolver and shot Eames twice. After Eames died from his wounds, Higman was tried and acquitted on a plea of self-defense.

The Eames Vacuum Brake Company continued to make braking equipment until 1890, when the New York Air Brake Company took over the plant on Beebee's Island. During the Eames years, brakes had been built by the company for 29 railways in the United States, Canada, Cuba, Brazil and Great Britain.

The New York Air Brake Company continued operations on Beebee's Island and on the mainland at Factory Street for ten years. In 1901, the company purchased 250 acres of land near Pearl Street on the outskirts of Watertown and completed an immense plant by 1910.

The company has been a pioneer from the start in the development of braking equipment. The AB brake has been a tremendous boon to railroads, for each unit is designed and made to be completely interchangeable with every other unit and with units made by other manufacturers, thus minimizing repair problems. The Air Brake also has developed an electric-pneumatic type of brake suitable for use by diesel engines in streamlined trains running at high speeds. Many high-speed freight and passenger locomotives are equipped with automatic controls which will set if the engineer leaves his post or becomes ill. Other brakes set automatically if the air line between two cars comes apart, and thus bring the train to a halt.

During World War II, Air Brake purchased the Hydraulic Pump Company of Chicago, and began the manufacture of hydraulic piston-type pumps for military installation. Since that time, though the company continues to make air brakes, it has expanded more and more into the hydraulic pump field.

XIV
THE FARMERS GO TO MARKET

THE PHENOMENAL GROWTH of industry along the Black River and its tributaries could not have taken place without the assistance of farmers, who fed the ever-increasing population, and villages, which supplied stores, banks, professional services and educational facilities.

This interdependence of industry, agriculture and commerce demanded better lines of communication. Roads were needed to reach the river and bridges to cross it. Leaders, soon after 1800, began to pound the drum for a main road through the Black River country. Jacob Brown of Brownville, Henry H. Coffeen of Watertown, William Henderson of Henderson, Walter Martin of Martinsburg, Augustus Sacket of Sackets Harbor and Philip Ten Eyck of Champion were all instrumental in securing the military road known as the State Road, which was built by money raised under the State Lottery Act of 1803.

The State Road passed through Turin, Martinsburg, Lowville, Champion, Rutland and Watertown on its way to Brownville and Sackets Harbor. It was not a good road, but it handled troop movements during the War of 1812 and brought mail service and stagecoach lines to the North Country. Ela Merriam carried the mail every day but Sunday for 36 years "over as muddy a road as could be found in the state," according to Dr. Hough, who knew whereof he spoke, for he had to use the road. The record trip for stages took place on February 19, 1829. Though snow lay two and a half feet deep that day, and 39 minutes were consumed in stops to pick up mail, the 93 miles from Utica to Sackets Harbor were covered in nine hours and 45 minutes.

Privately-owned plank roads, with toll gates at intervals, took over briefly during the middle of the nineteenth century, but they never got a foothold in the North Country. Many failed before going into operation; others, faced with the high cost of maintenance, due chiefly to deterioration of the planks, soon called it a day. The Black River region went back to the dirt road, though a McAdamized road had been recommended as early as 1842. These dirt roads were muddy in spring, dusty in summer and sometimes impassable in winter, but their vast network provided farmers with access to the villages and to the river.

Folks had to cross the river, so bridges became necessities. Brownville, which played second fiddle to Watertown in most enterprises, had Deacon Oliver Bartholomew build a bridge in 1802, a year before Henry Coffeen threw a rude span across the river below the Great Falls at Watertown. Two bridges later crossed the river at Watertown, one at Factory Square and a second over the cascade at Mill Street. The latter bridge was replaced in 1853 by the iron suspension bridge which became the wonder of the North Country. Great Bend, at the crossing of an important early route, built a bridge in 1804 and Felt's Mills got one five years later. Carthage, served by Judge Nathan Ford's Oswegatchie Road from Louisville, replaced Bossuot's ferry with a bridge in 1812. A few years later, Joseph Budd built five bridges across the islands from West Carthage to Carthage, but they soon went out of use. A bridge was raised on the site of the first bridge in 1829; this bridge served the public until the State, as part of the Black River Canal project, constructed a sturdy bridge in 1853.

The long, calm stretch from Carthage to Lyons Falls depended upon ferries until 1828, when Thomas Puffer of Watson built a bridge across the river, connecting his town with Lowville. Nelson J. Beach had Puffer rebuild this bridge with a draw four years later in anticipation of the canal. In waiting for the canal, the bridge deteriorated, so a new Beach's Bridge

A Touch of New England at Lowville. State Street and Presbyterian Church. Fynmore Photo.

Is Beach's Bridge Open? Not during the early weeks of April. Fynmore Photo.

The T. B. Basselin Mansion at Croghan, showing the "sentinel lions."
Photo courtesy Gerald Spencer.

Industries on the Beaver at Beaver Falls. Beaverite, Latex and J. P.
Lewis Co. Fynmore Photo.

was built in 1851. The State provided the piers, abutments and draw, while the superstructure was paid for by taxes raised in the two towns. Thomas Puffer also built, in 1833, the Illingworth Bridge near New Bremen. The Parker Bridge, from Castorland to Naumberg, went up at State expense in 1865. Tiffany's Landing Bridge near Glensdale (Glenfield) was built in 1846, and was the covered bridge which was torn down to permit the "L. R. Lyon" to make its maiden voyage down the river. Caleb Lyon spanned the Moose River at Lyonsdale in 1820, and Port Leyden got a bridge three years later. Lyon built a bridge below the High Falls in 1824 and one above the falls in 1836.

The most unique bridge across the Black River was built at the confluence of that stream with the Moose at Lyons Falls in 1849. This wooden "three-way" bridge left Lyons Falls "all in one piece"; halfway across the Black, it spread into two forks, one spanning the Black, the other the Moose. It was not a covered bridge, but high guard rails prevented folks from dropping off into the rivers. The bridge served Lyons Falls, Lyonsdale and Greig for 67 years. It was replaced by the present iron "three-way" bridge in 1916. Practical jokers, in directing strangers from Lyons Falls to Greig, still enjoy telling their unsuspecting victims to "turn left at the middle of the bridge."

Though roads and bridges had been improved and the canal was booming, the Black River country had to wait a long time for a railroad. The Black River and Utica Railroad got as far as Boonville in 1855, reached Lowville in 1867, Carthage in 1871 and Clayton in 1873. Travellers could change cars at Carthage and take the Carthage & Sackets Harbor Railroad to Watertown, which had had rail service since 1851, when the first train of the Watertown and Rome arrived from Adams to a tumult of cheers.

Lowville, Carthage and Watertown were the chief recipients of these improvements in transportation. Lowville did not have much to offer in the way of industry and its only accesses to the river were at Spofford's Landing and Smith's Landing, but it was the marketing center for potatoes, some hops, and dairy products, including the famous Lewis County cheese. After years of trying, it pried the county seat away from Martinsburg in 1864. Six years later, it got the Kellogg House, which rose from the ashes of the earlier Bostwick House on the main street. The Kellogg House, an imposing four-story building, was the pride of Lowville. What other hotel in the North Country could boast that the floor of its office had been laid in pure marble?

Farmers could satisfy all of their needs in Lowville, which had two solid banks, two barbers, four bookstores, four carriage-makers, four clothing stores, seven dry goods emporia, eight grocery stores, four hardware shops, four milliners and three photographers. If professional services were needed, Lowville could provide three dentists, eight physicians and fifteen lawyers. For entertainment, there was the Ruscoe Opera House. Guests at the Kellogg House did not have to wet their feet to go to "the opera," for a door led from the hotel to the place of entertainment.

Disastrous fires played a large part in the evolution of both Watertown and Carthage. Early settlers feared fire more than storms, floods or Indians. When the village of Watertown was incorporated, on April 5, 1816, five fire wardens were elected, each of whom was supplied with four ladders. Each owner or occupant of a building was obliged to furnish one or two buckets. Any male over 15 was subject to a one dollar fine if he did not put himself under the direction of the fire wardens after a fire alarm. These wardens carried white staffs so that they might be distinguished. The bucket-brigades were a beginning. Volunteer fire companies were soon organized. Watertown had five, each with a steam engine. Carthage boasted three. Hydrants were placed in strategic places in these villages.

It was the Watertown volunteer firemen who battled the serious fire of May 13, 1849, which wiped out the business section of the village. It taught the volunteer firemen, who had been jealous of each other, that there was strength in unity, so the Watertown Fire Department was chartered by an act of the State Legislature on April 10, 1850.

Carthage had been plagued by fire since July 15, 1861, when twenty buildings in the business section of the village burned at a loss of $60,000. Another fire, later in that year, plus conflagrations in 1872 and 1874, resulted in terrific loss of property, and the 1874 fire cost one human life. The volunteers organized as the Carthage Fire Department on April 27, 1875.

The morning of October 20, 1884 broke clear and sunny, and a brisk breeze blew along the Black River between Carthage and West Carthage. There had been little rain that fall, and the wooden buildings along the waterfront on both sides of the river were bone dry. When the fire alarm sounded, the Carthage Fire Department crossed the bridge to West Carthage to fight a fire which had started in a sash and blind factory, had spread to a tub factory and a furniture factory and was eating into a pile of hemlock bark owned by a tannery. The whole West Carthage waterfront was soon a mass of flames, and sparks ignited buildings on Guyot Island and Furnace Island.

While the Carthage firemen were striving manfully to extinguish these fires, the wind suddenly veered to the north, blew sparks across the river, and started fires in West Street in Carthage.

A hurry call was sent to the Watertown, Lowville and Boonville fire companies. Watertown arrived at one o'clock by train, with a steamer, 1,000 feet of hose and 30 experienced firemen. Lowville's La France steamer pulled in soon afterward, while Boonville landed during the afternoon.

Water in the hydrants gave out, so the firemen had to use the Black River to supply the steamers. Chief Engineer William H. Cole of Watertown took charge. He stationed the Carthage pumper at the foot of State Street to pump water from the river and relay it to the Watertown steamer, which was located in the middle of State Street. The Lowville and Boonville departments fought fires along the waterfront in the northeasterly section of the village. This first experiment in mutual aid succeeded in getting the fire under control by five o'clock, but the fire had spread over 70 acres. One hundred homes and 57 other structures had been demolished, including all the schools and four churches. The loss was estimated at between $500,000 and $750,000.

The 1849 fire in Watertown had been a cruel blow, but, in a way, it may have been a good thing for that village. The destroyed buildings, mostly of wood, had been unsightly and outmoded. The new Watertown business district, built chiefly of brick and stone, had attractiveness and permanence. Carthage, before its fire, had been one of the shabbiest settlements in the North Country. The waterfront had contained many dilapidated wooden structures and even State Street could boast of few attractive buildings. Carthage, even more so than Watertown, "rose from its ashes." Attractive churches added their spires to the skyline, a new high school building became the pride of the village, and wide State Street, with its new Strickland Building and other modern brick structures, became a shopping center where practically any product could be purchased amid pleasant surroundings.

If one said, "All roads lead to Watertown," he would not be far from the truth, for, like ancient Rome, Watertown was the hub from which roads and railroads radiated in all directions. Watertown could outdo Lowville, Carthage and other villages in services to visitors. Space does not permit listing the 18 hotels, the countless stores, the important banks and the plethora of professional services. A mention of a few must suffice.

The leading hostelry, the Woodruff House, raised in 1851, fronted on the Public Square. Its 90 rooms were the latest in comfort, and the pillared dining room compared favorably with that of the Astor House in New York City. It was a hotel for "swells," and country folk could not afford to stay there. Most farmers congregated at the Harris House, an old wooden building across the Public Square, where they could eat ample meals and have comfortable rooms without having their countrified manners embarrass them in front of the tight-trousered gentlemen and hoop-skirted ladies who ate in the dining room at the Woodruff House.

The shopping center for farmers was the Paddock Arcade on Washington Street. This fabulous building was a world in itself, for it contained the post office, the telegraph office, ten stores and a large saloon. And it was a treat to see it at night, illuminated by the new-fangled gas from the Watertown Gas-Light Co.

Farmers who stayed over night at the Harris House might pick up a copy of any one of five Watertown newspapers and read for a spell before attending an entertainment at Washington Hall or the City Opera House. And, in the fall, there was always the Jefferson County Fair, which had been started by James Le Ray de Chaumont.

Yes, Watertown had everything—a road and railroad center, thriving industries along the river, excellent hotels, the best stores in the North Country, and plenty of entertainment.

Watertown had nobody to blame but itself for a situation of which it was justly proud. It had survived industrial failure, a fire which had wiped out its business center, a disastrous flood, and other roadblocks which might have downed a less enterprising village. And, by 1869, it had taken on the status of the first city in the North Country.

The outstanding observation one might make about Watertown seems to be the fact that everything was accomplished without going outside for capital. The pioneers had made money, and they were willing to invest it in enterprises which would make for a better Watertown.

This growth of capital created a need for banking facilities. No one community could undertake the project in 1816, so the Jefferson County Bank, incorporated in that year with a capital of $400,000 in shares of $50 each, had to be sponsored by investors all over Jefferson County. A committee was appointed to apportion the stock and to choose a site for the bank. Here the rivalry between Brownville and Watertown flamed anew. The thirteen towns represented on the committee were Adams, Antwerp, Brownville, Champion, Ellisburg, Henderson, Hounsfield, Le Ray, Lorraine, Rodman, Rutland, Watertown and Wilna. John Paddock, the representative from Brownville, knowing he could not get the bank for his village and not wanting Watertown to have it, swayed enough votes to get the bank located in Adams. He also became its first president. The move backfired. The bank did not succeed and closed its doors in 1819. Five years later, it started anew in Watertown, erected a new building, and became the backbone of North Country financial life.

Watertown gained other banks as the years went on—the Bank of Watertown, the Watertown Bank and Loan Company, the Merchants' Exchange Bank, the Black River Bank and the Union Bank. Two private banks, Henry Keep's Bank and Wooster Sherman's Bank, along with the Black River Bank, were destroyed in the fire of 1849. A savings bank entered the picture in 1859, with the organization of the Jefferson County Savings Bank. After the act creating national banks, in 1865, the Jefferson County Bank assumed that status, as did the National Union Bank. Two new organizations joined them, the City National Bank and the Watertown National Bank.

Sackets Harbor made an effort to get into the banking business in 1834 with the Sackets Harbor Bank. Though backed by such substantial citizens as Henry H. Coffeen of Watertown and Noadiah Hubbard of Champion, it lasted but 18 years. In 1852, E. B. Camp started the State Bank at the Harbor. Over in Adams, the Hungerford Bank opened its doors in 1845. Hiram D. McCollum's Bank of Carthage started in 1853 and the First National Bank of Brownville in

1866. By 1893, Clayton boasted two banks, the Exchange Bank, which had merged with the Bank of Clayton, and the First National Bank of Clayton, which was an offshoot of the earlier Citizens' Bank.

Martinsburg, the first county seat of Lewis County, opened a bank in 1833. Though blessed with the support of John W. Martin, Isaac W. Bostwick, S. D. Hungerford, Lyman R. Lyman and Ela N. Merriam, its career came to a close in 1854. The Bank of Lowville, organized in 1838, had a hectic time. The Panic of 1857 caused its temporary suspension and $6,000 was stolen from its safes four years later. James L. Leonard saved the bank during these crises and also during a greater one during the Civil War. At the time of his death, in 1867, he was planning a new bank building at the corner of State Street and Shady Avenue. The act of 1865 solved Lowville's banking problems, for the village gained two strong banks, the First National Bank and the Black River National Bank.

Lowville was the first North Country village to do something about educating boys and girls beyond the district schools. When Lewis County was established in 1805, Lowville was so confident that it would be the county seat that it put up, at the head of its main street, a building to house the government. The subscription to raise money read in part: "It is contemplated to build a house which may serve for religious worship, or any other public meeting, as also for an academy." Silas Stow, Isaac W. Bostwick, Daniel Kelley and other leading citizens allowed that, if Lowville could not be the county seat, it might become an educational center. They hired Rev. Isaac Clinton to teach a classical school in the new building, and sent a petition to the Board of Regents for permission to start an academy. The charter for Lowville Academy arrived in 1808 and the school became the first private academy in the North Country.

Lowville Academy had its ups and downs. Samuel W. Taylor, who became principal in 1817, wanted to convert the academy into a boarding school with dormitories. The trustees vetoed that idea, but consented to erect a new academy in line with Taylor's educational specifications. The result was a twelve-sided stone atrocity with a wooden attic surmounted by a tin dome and a bell cupola. Taylor had intended the cubicles in the attic for use as dormitory rooms; instead, they became study rooms. Taylor brought down on his shoulders the wrath of students, trustees and parents by his strict disciplinary methods and continual spying tactics. When the critics said his methods might make boys of men, but would never make men of boys, Taylor resigned in a huff. The building disintegrated rapidly and had to be torn down in 1836, five years after Taylor left Lowville. The people of the village lost a good man in Taylor, who went on to be president of Lewisburgh University (Bucknell) and Madison University (Colgate).

A new Lowville Academy, built on the site of the first building, was a three-story brick structure to which wings were added in 1861. The academy never became a boarding school, though many of the students boarded in the village. Some of them were "cheese-box boarders," poor boys and girls who brought a week's supply of food from home in cheese-boxes. Others were children of wealthy people. Mme. de Feriet thought so highly of the school that she brought her nephew, Gabriel, up from New Orleans so that he could be educated at Lowville Academy.

Watertown's maiden attempts at establishing academies did not turn out too well. A school building was put up in 1810, was taken over as a hospital during the War of 1812, and dismantled a few years later. Watertown Academy, started with considerable idealism and with a stone building "standing in a pleasant grove near the village," never got accredited by the Board of Regents.

A statement in the 1832 prospectus of Watertown Academy indicated the feelings of its sponsors toward education: "It has long been a subject of reproach to our community, that, while other interests are flourishing, the interests of education were neglected. Among us there has been no seminary for the education of boys, above the ordinary district school, and the consequence has been, that parents have sent their children abroad, at a very heavy expense, or brought them up in comparative ignorance at home."

Watertown Academy bowed out in 1841 in favor of the Black River Literary and Religious Institute, a school backed by the Watertown Presbytery and the Black River Association. Religious overtones could be found in the prospectus, a part of which read: "We need a school in which the authenticity and inspiration of the Bible shall be taught; in which the truths and duties of the Christian religion shall be inculcated, and in which moral virtues may be cultivated in such a way as to form a dignified character, guarded against the errors and vices of the world, in which our children shall have all the security thrown around them that they can enjoy under the pious and parental roof." To make sure that these virtues were preserved, boys and girls were to be in separate departments and half of the faculty of 12 were to be ministers.

A stone and brick building went up in 1838 at the corner of State and Mechanic streets and the school received its first visitation from the Regents later in that year. The strict religious atmosphere was softened in 1846, when the name of the school was changed to Jefferson County Institute and only the principal had to be a minister or a member of the Congregational or the Presbyterian church. Enrollment increased from 204 in 1846 to 512 in 1853. The Institute became part of the Watertown public school system in 1865.

A rash of small academies broke out over the North Country. Carthage Academy, one of the larger ones, operated for about twenty-five years and was absorbed by the public high school in 1866. Three rivals to Lowville Academy sputtered and failed: Turin's attempt never got off the ground; Denmark operated a little wooden academy between 1829 and 1850; and, by a queer reversal of history, when the county seat at Martinsburg was shifted to Lowville in 1864, the courthouse at Martinsburg became Martin Institute. Brownville had a Female Seminary for a few years and La Fargeville's attempt at higher education, Orleans Academy, had the most hectic career of all, for its first wooden building was flattened by a North Country gale and its replacement did not endure.

Three boarding academies flourished in the North Country during the second half of the nineteenth century. The Antwerp Literary Institute, after an uncertain passage since 1813, merged with the Governeur Wesleyan Seminary in 1874 to become the Ives Seminary. Belleville Union Academy got under way in 1829 and weathered two crises, the first during the Panic of 1857, the second when the male population marched off to fight in the Civil War. The academy had a boom year in 1866, when it enrolled 342 students, but by 1893, the school housed but 100 boys and girls. Belleville was the scene of one of the first experiments in vocational education. An early principal built a shop beside the stone academy and encouraged boys to learn practical trades. The project failed when the farm boys would have no part of it. At Adams, the Hungerford Collegiate Institute drew students from all over the North Country between the end of the Civil War and the close of the nineteenth century. The school nearly passed out of existence in 1882, when its imposing building was put up for sale to pay school debts. It was saved through efforts of local citizens and graduates, and reopened its doors that same year under the name of Adams Collegiate Institute, with the aim: "to make men and women out of our students."

These private academies turned out many leaders in the Black River country and served a definite purpose in the advancement of the region. At the fiftieth anniversary of the opening of Lowville Academy, an imposing list of former students came to Lowville, including Nelson J. Beach, the canal commissioner, Charles Dayan, the legislator who had been instrumental in securing the canal, Dr. Franklin B. Hough, Lyman R. Lyman, the largest land-owner in Lewis County, Charles A. Mann, agent for the Holland Land Company, and Harvey P. Willard, a school teacher who was soon to become proprietor and editor of the *Black River Herald* at Boonville.

The trend away from private academies and toward public high schools resulted in the closing of some academies and the conversion of others into public-supported institutions. It is interesting to note that two of the big central schools in the North Country today are Belleville Union Academy and Central School and Lowville Academy and Central School. Folks have not forgotten.

XV
"WHITE COAL"

INDEPENDENCE DAY fell on a Sunday in 1880, so the villages in the Black River country celebrated the holiday on Monday, the 5th. There were the usual parades, speeches and firecrackers and, in villages which could afford them, displays of fireworks in the evening.

Watertown staged a great show that year. In addition to the usual attractions, the city engaged Nellie Thurston of Prospect, billed as "the only female aeronaut in America," to make a balloon ascension from the Public Square. Nellie sailed off into the "wild blue yonder" at 5:20 P.M., to the gasps and cheers of thousands. Inasmuch as the fair Nellie had landed in the Adirondack wilderness after an ascension from Carthage the previous September, folks prayed that their favorite would not have to endure another night alone with the bears and panthers, an experience which she had described with embellishments for the newspapers.

Whereas Nellie's feat represented the passing of an era, the exhibition of electric lighting in the evening foretold a future when electricity made from water power would provide comfort and convenience, not only to industry along the river, but to farmers living in the most isolated areas of the North Country.

Watertown's streets, business establishments and some homes had been illuminated by gas since 1852, when F. T. Story organized the Watertown Gas-Light Company. Electricity was something brand new, for Thomas A. Edison had demonstrated his first incandescent lamp on Dec. 21, 1879.

The man who brought the electrical demonstration to Watertown on July 5, 1880 was Timothy Teall of Syracuse. He installed four large arc lamps: three of them were to light up the Public Square and the business section; the fourth, a rotating lamp, was placed atop the Woodruff House, so that its rays could reach the surrounding hills.

The demonstration turned out to be an unqualified success. The Public Square was so well-lighted that folks claimed that they could see a pin dropped at their feet. People aided by the revolving lamp read newspapers by its light.

Watertown had to wait for five years before acquiring permanent electric lights. George D. Allen of the Excelsior Electric Light Company of New York came to Watertown, established headquarters at the Woodruff House, and canvassed the business houses. After he had secured 15 customers, using 25 lamps, he installed a dynamo in the Knowlton Brothers mill and strung wires to his customers. As an advertisement, he put up three lights on the Public Square, so that Watertown folks could see for themselves how much better his lights were than the ones operated by the Watertown Gas-Light Company. Watertown liked Allen's lights, so he sold them to the city, which contracted for eight more. The lights were operated until 10 P.M. in summer and until midnight in winter. The Excelsior company moved out of the Knowlton Brothers mill and installed its dynamo in an old stone building it had rented on the river bank near Beebee's Island.

Businessmen of Watertown, enthusiastic about the lights, organized a stock company to purchase the plant and business of the Excelsior company. Watertown, as was its custom, moved with lightning speed. The first lights had been installed by Excelsior in late May. On August 11th, the Watertown Electric Light Company, Ltd. was formed. The certificate of incorporation, signed by the Secretary of State, was recorded in the office of the Jefferson county clerk on Aug. 27th. The plant of the Excelsior company, together with its lighting contract with the city, was turned over to the Watertown Electric Light Company, Ltd. on Sept. 1st.

Watertown had three lighting systems in 1886. There were 203 oil lamps still in use. The Watertown Gas-Light Company, which had served the city for 34 years, provided 113 lamps. Though the new electric light company had but 20 arc lights, it became obvious that the earlier lighting systems would lose out to the arc lights. The city council, by a 4 to 3 vote, entered into a seven year contract with the Watertown Electric Light Company, Ltd. on October 22nd to supply 75 lamps of 2,000 candle power at $68 per lamp. Foreseeing this result, the electric light company had purchased the Cataract flouring mill from Eli and Harriet E. Settle. A stone building was put up on the site in 1891.

The Watertown Gas-Light Company and the Watertown Electric Light Company, Ltd. shared the lighting of Watertown until they were both absorbed by the Watertown Light and Power Company, in 1909 and 1907, respectively.

The Watertown experience is typical of early hydro-electric developments along the Black River and its tributaries; it, like the others, was purely local, with little thought of extending operations beyond the borders of its particular community. Small electric light companies sprang up all over the North Country. Some were operated by private corporations, others by municipalities. Some mills along the rivers installed electric plants to serve their particular industries. Forestport and Boonville started municipal plants. The Lowville Electric Light and Power Co. got under way in 1889. The Campbell Transmission Co. and the Dexter Light and Power Co. Inc. provided electricity for mills at the mouth of the river. Charles Pratt, the lumber and paper-making tycoon, put up a small plant on the Deer River near Copenhagen. A plant on Otter Creek provided electricity for Glenfield.

Two hydro-electric plants were built on the Beaver River: the Carthage Electric Light Co., run by the Strickland family, put up a plant at Effley Falls; Lafayette Wetmore of the Wetmore Electric Co. absorbed the Lowville firm and built at Belfort. Both firms were absorbed by the Northern New York Utilities in 1914. It is said that Wetmore, in creating a lake at Belfort, had neglected to buy up the land he had inundated. Northern New York Utilities, aware of this oversight, purchased the land and told Wetmore to get his water off it.

The Watertown Electric Light Company, Ltd., under the presidency of DeWitt C. Middleton, had the field to itself until 1904, when John Byron Taylor purchased the Watertown Gas-Light Company. Taylor envisioned power development on a large scale. He bought the Remington pulp mill and water power at Black River, with the intention of building an electric plant to compete with the Watertown Electric Light Company, Ltd. He bought out that company in 1906, and by 1915 gained approval of the Public Service Commission to create the Northern New York Utilities. One by one, he absorbed the privately and municipally owned plants at Cape Vincent, Chaumont, Dexter, Forestport and Port Leyden, in addition to the Wetmore holdings at Belfort and Lowville, and the Strickland plant at Effley Falls.

Taylor passed out of the hydro-electric picture in 1920, when he sold his properties to a syndicate which included Floyd L. Carlisle of the St. Regis Paper Company and representatives of the J. P. Lewis Paper Company of Beaver Falls, the Remington Paper & Power Company, the Champion Paper Company, the Taggarts Paper Company, the Harmon Paper Company of Brownville and the Warren Parchment Company of Dexter.

The Northern New York Utilities, under the leadership of Taylor and later of Carlisle, gained almost a monopoly on water power sites on the Black and Beaver rivers. On the Beaver, they improved the Wetmore plant at Belfort and built six other power plants along the river—Taylorville, Elmer Falls, Effley Falls, Soft Maple, Eagle Falls and Moshier. Water power on the Black was utilized by plants at Herrings, Deferiet, Black River and at Diamond Island, Sewall's Island and Beebee's Island in Watertown. Outside the jurisdiction of the Utilities were the two J. P. Lewis Paper Company plants at High Falls and at Beaver Falls on the Beaver, the Gould Paper Company development at Gouldtown on the Moose, the Boonville municipal plant on the Black, plus some small operations at mills along the rivers.

The Utilities ran into an obstacle in Watertown, where it had been supplying lights for the city and wished to continue to do so. Watertown, under its first city manager, Clarence A. Bingham, and its public-spirited mayor, Robert E. Cahill, completed its municipally-owned hydro-electric plant at Delano Island in 1924. The Utilities wanted to lease the plant from the city and provide lighting at a cost of $60,000 per year. The city refused the offer, and the Utilities had to settle for a contract entitling them to purchase surplus power from the city.

The Northern Utilities consolidated in 1937 with the Niagara Hudson Public Service Corporation, which changed its name in that same year to the Central New York Power Corporation. In 1950, the name became Niagara-Mohawk Power Corporation, a tremendous utilities operation which supplies most of the power and lighting facilities, not only for the North Country, but for much of the State.

Watertown and Boonville have their municipal plants, and

some mills and a few small operators like Raymond Bailey at Port Leyden and Raymond Frank at Dexter manufacture electric power and sell it to Niagara-Mohawk. The Gould Paper Company on the Moose at Gouldtown and the J. P. Lewis Paper Company at High Falls and Beaver Falls on the Beaver, provide their own power, sell excess power to Niagara-Mohawk, and are supplied by that company when requirements exceed generation capabilities of their private plants.

Electricity has proved to be a boon to the people of the Black River country. Industries along the Black River and its tributaries can operate more efficiently during time of low water. Farmers use electricity to operate pumps, milking machines and other agricultural machines. Homes have been brightened by electric lighting and electrical appliances have eased the labors of housewives. Farmers have been brought into contact with the outside world through the media of radio and television.

The Black River and its tributaries had made one more contribution to the welfare of the people.

XVI
THE RIVER TAKES OVER

THE BLACK RIVER and its tributaries reacted to the harness like a stallion and a herd of two-year-olds. At certain seasons, they proved to be good roadsters, carrying on at an even pace and providing water power for the mills which occupied their banks. Spring brought out all the friskiness in their makeups. When the hand of winter let go its grasp in the Adirondacks, they champed at the bit and poured uncontrollable quantities of coffee-colored water through their narrow, rocky channels. These floods aided lumbermen, who could run their logs down the tributaries to the sawmills, but they wreaked havoc on dams, bridges and mills which impeded their paths. And, from Lyons Falls to Carthage, finding no place to go, the turbulent water overflowed the channel of the Black River and created a lake which at times measured 30 miles in length. Mid-summer brought a change in the character of the river and its tributaries. They responded to the hot, dry weather by lying down in harness. Industry, deprived of adequate water, had to operate on a curtailed schedule or shut down entirely.

The people of the North Country, though grateful for the water power which had turned the wheels of industry since the days of the first settlers, became frightened and irritated at the capricious streams to which they owed their livelihood.

Floods plagued the Black River valley from the beginning. Though little is known about the early floods, Dr. Hough reported that the worst one up to 1860 occurred in 1807, and that the river went on other rampages in 1818, 1833, 1839, 1841 and 1843. This last flood wiped out William Huntington's thriving sawmill at Huntingtonville near Watertown. Great Bend lost its first sawmill in the flood of 1807 and, in the spring of 1862, while spectators at Great Bend were standing on the bridge watching the flood waters, an old, deserted mill was loosened from its foundations. It came hurtling down the stream and crashed with full force against the bridge. The panic-stricken spectators scurried for shore. Two young boys were swept away with the bridge and the mill. One succeeded in reaching land several miles down the river, but the other was drowned.

Dr. Hough, the sagacious observer, wrote: "This river has proved somewhat subject to floods, which requires the exercise of care in locating buildings upon its banks; but, from its bed being generally rock, ample means are available for the security of dams which have been seldom or never swept off." And it is true that, though bridges and mills have been swept away by floods, the timber-crib dams have usually survived.

When the Black River Canal was constructed, water had to be impounded so that it could be released to supply the canal during the summer months. A diversionary dam was built at Forestport to send water to the canal at Boonville, and three reservoirs about 20 miles up the river were created to impound water. To improve navigation for steamboats between Lyons Falls and Carthage, a dam was put up at the latter village. These measures were taken merely to bring water to the canal. Nothing further was done to control the river in time of flood or drouth.

Dr. Hough wrote, in 1854: "From the extent and number of lakes that exist near the sources of this river, and its tributaries, in the primary regions of Lewis and Herkimer counties, no apprehension need be felt that the opposite extreme of drouth will necessarily occur in the future, for, by constructing dams and sluices at the outlets of these lakes, they may be cheaply converted into immense reservoirs to retain the spring floods resulting from the melting of winter snows, and equalize the discharge through the dry season; thus serving the double purpose of preventing excessive freshets, or extreme drouth."

Dr. Hough's advice was not taken. Bad floods in 1857 and 1862 caused considerable destruction, and mill-wheels did not budge during dry seasons.

Snow lay deep in the Adirondacks in 1869, so folks became concerned about flood. G. H. P. Gould of Lyons Falls reported on January 2nd: "The reservoirs need repairs on the north and south branches. The top timbers to the walls are so much decayed that the shackels to the gates are loose, making it difficult to work them; the two or three courses of timber should be replaced. The entire timber work at the sides of the outlet of the Woodhull reservoir has failed and must be rebuilt, or what would be better, filled with embankment."

Spring was late that year, but it came with a suddenness which released the pent-up energies of rivers all over New

York. The Hudson went on one of its worst rampages in late April. A boom above the dam at Glens Falls burst, sending 40,000 logs hurtling toward the capital district, where the river front streets in Albany and Troy could be navigated only by boats. The Mohawk and its tributaries entered into competition. The Mohawk valley became one long lake from Rome to Schenectady. No trains ran from Syracuse to Albany for several days, for the tracks between St. Johnsville and Fonda lay under several feet of water.

The people of the Black River valley did not find this news consoling. The water had been high, but it seemed to be abating; yet folks had their fingers crossed, for they had had long experience with the capriciousness of their river.

Late in the afternoon of April 21st, 1869, a rider dashed into Forestport to warn the people that a wall of water was bearing down on the village from North Lake, where the dam had burst. Men were alerted and crews worked frantically to buttress the Forestport dam, which was holding back huge rafts of logs and spars. Their labors proved useless, for the surge of water hit the rafts with terrific force. The logs were ground together and thrown end-over-end toward the dam. Sixty-foot spruce spars snapped like pipe-stems. An eye-witness reported: "The logs seemed to be fighting each other, and when caught in the drift, would be almost instantly stripped of their bark, twisted, split, and broken like straws." With a crash that sounded louder than the roar of the river, they hit the dam, tore away 120 feet of it, and careened downstream, digging out a 40-foot channel, taking away a gristmill and a hub factory, and badly damaging several sawmills. Forestport's loss in buildings and lumber was estimated at from $30,000 to $40,000.

The river rushed toward Lyons Falls at a frantic pace, carrying with it thousands of logs. En route, it took away the bridge and a sawmill at Hawkinsville, and flooded the Eureka Tannery of Anderson Bros. A man was carried downstream with the bridge, but he managed to reach shore a half mile below, wet and alive, but badly frightened. Dewey's mill at Port Leyden was swept away and the Snyder Bros. tannery was practically inundated. By the time the flood met the roaring Moose at Lyons Falls, it was over 30 feet deep. It poured 600 million cubic feet of water over the falls and rushed on toward Carthage. Part of the State dam at that village had been swept away a few days earlier, so the mass of water pressed relentlessly on toward Watertown, which it reached at about five o'clock the next morning, after raising havoc all along the river from Carthage.

The inhabitants of Watertown had gone to bed the night before, secure in their minds that the danger of flood had passed. The roar of the Great Falls got them up early, for it was louder than Niagara, or what they thought Niagara to be. Almost the entire population of the village—it was to become a city a little over two weeks later—lined the river banks and the high bridges to get a view of the spectacle.

John A. Haddock, who witnessed the flood at Watertown, wrote: "Thousands of people flocked to the banks of Black River on the forenoon of April 22nd, to gaze upon the sublime spectacle. One of the most imposing sights of the many presented by that raging flood was to be seen between the Knowltons' paper-mill and Lord's factory, where a volume of water like an improvised Niagara poured through, half as high as the buildings. It was curious how it walled itself up in such a way, explainable only by the velocity of the current and the tremendous force behind it. It was an inspiring and a thrilling sight, not soon effaced from the beholder's memory."

The flood might have been "inspiring" and "thrilling" to a spectator, but it proved disastrous for industries along the river at Watertown. Gilderoy Lord's iron works were swept away, as were several small gristmills and sawmills. Moulton & Herrick's mill, completely undermined, hung over the river, supported by cables. Knowlton Brothers lost the foundation of a new addition to their paper mill. Farwell & Baker's tannery was filled with water. Kimball's barley mill, which was badly damaged, was consumed by fire a few days later, along with Pratt's cotton mill. The estimated loss in Watertown was $250,000. Four timber crib dams, built in 1803, 1805, 1814 and 1835, survived the flood.

A reporter from the *Utica Morning Herald* was sent to describe the flood at Watertown. He did so in detail, and added: "The sight up and down the river is one of terrific grandeur, equalling the St. Lawrence in her famous Long Sault and Lachine rapids."

The flood created havoc from North Lake to Dexter. Dams, bridges and mills were swept away. The Forestport feeder became a raging torrent, causing considerable damage to the Black River Canal above and below Boonville. The flats from Lyons Falls to Carthage were littered with logs, spars and debris. At Watertown, industry came to a halt for several weeks. The tanneries were flooded, the flouring mills could not operate, and a ruined flume shut down the Portable Steam Engine Company. Breaks in the railroad bed between Lyons Falls and Lowville stopped train service for over a week.

A few days after the flood, a story trickled through from Forestport which threw the whole Black River valley into a rage. The *Utica Morning Herald* reported: "This winter, for political consideration Mr. Dawson, who had been in charge of the reservoirs for several years, was removed and a new man placed in charge who knew nothing of the importance of protecting this work against spring floods."

Though heavy rains had caused the North Lake reservoir to rise, the "political appointee" had not taken the precaution of opening the gates and releasing the excess water. The dam, which was in need of repair, simply gave way.

There were about 300 mill-owners between Forestport and Dexter, and nearly all of them had suffered losses from the flood. Damage suits against the State poured into the courts; 2,370 claimants sued for a total of $700,000. Some were nuisance claims with no basis, but the serious ones brought awards of about $450,000 to the claimants. The cases dragged on for years, the last one being settled in 1892.

The State's defense was based on the contention that the damage below Carthage had been caused by the usual spring flood, which had begun to recede when the North Lake dam gave way. Their lawyers maintained that the mass of water let loose from the reservoir could not have reached Watertown in 12 to 14 hours. The claimants based their arguments on testimony of hydraulic engineers, who said that when the "wave of transmission" of the large mass of water which entered the 40-odd mile stretch below Lyons Falls reached Carthage, it would be kept up as long as the force was applied, which would be until the North Lake reservoir had emptied itself.

The flood of 1869, the most disastrous in the history of the Black River to date, did not stir the State to take Dr. Hough's advice. A few gestures were made. The dams at North Lake and at Forestport were rebuilt and a new dam to impound water was constructed above Forestport in 1894. In an attempt to compensate for loss of water being diverted out of the Black River drainage area by the Erie and Black River Canals, the State built dams at Sixth Lake and Old Forge on the Moose in 1880, and a small reservoir at Stillwater on the Beaver in 1882.

Legislation favoring preservation of the Adirondacks took precedence over attempts at river control for the following thirty years. The "Forever Wild" amendment of 1885, strengthened in 1894 by the provision forbidding the sale, lease, exchange or destruction of lands in the Forest Preserve, not only curbed the lumbering interests at which it was aimed, but it also made control of the Black River and its tributaries virtually impossible. Any attempt by advocates of flood control to encroach on the Preserve was blocked by two powerful organizations, the New York Board of Trade and Transportation and the Association for the Protection of the Adirondacks, who felt that advocates of reservoirs within the Preserve, though talking about flood control and water pollution prevention, were more seriously interested in controlling the rivers for the development of hydro-electric power.

The Adirondack Park had been created by an act of the Legislature in 1892 and its exact boundaries were defined in the establishment of the Blue Line in 1904. The origin of this Blue Line goes back to 1884, when a map of State lands was drawn. In 1890, this map was reprinted. Two lines appeared, one in red to show the limits of the Forest Preserve, a second in blue outlining the boundaries of the proposed Adirondack Park, which had for its aim "a ground open for the free use of all the people for their health and pleasure" and also "the preservation of forest lands along the headwaters of the chief rivers of the state."

By the time the Blue Line was established, the lumbering interests had faded from the picture. They had never been interested in controlling the highs and lows of the Black River and its tributaries, for floods had aided them and drouths had not hurt them. Furthermore, they were still able to take timber from private lands within the Blue Line by buying from private owners, including the Adirondack League Club.

By 1904, the development of hydro-electric power had become essential to industries along the Black River and its tributaries, and every effort to establish flood control from that date has been inextricably bound up with what the advocates of forest preservation consider a "power grab."

The Board of Trade, in the previous year, had defeated the Lewis Water Storage Bill, which they called the "Grab Bill," claiming that it constituted a dangerous invasion of the Adirondack Preserve under the guise of preventing floods and freshets.

The first real test of water power rights came in 1905, before the recently created River Improvement Commission, when the Paul Smith's Electric Light and Power and Railroad Company petitioned the Commission for permission to dam the Saranac River on its own land at Franklin Falls and flood adjacent State land. The power company put emphasis on a dam which would control floods and prevent pollution in the river. The Board of Trade claimed that construction of such a dam would violate the "Forever Wild" amendment. The application of the power company was defeated in the Legislature as unconstitutional, but the Paul Smith's people went ahead and built dams at Franklin Falls and Union Falls on the Saranac River and flooded several hundred acres of State land. A suit against them was decided in their favor.

Two other reservoir projects, involving the new Barge Canal, were completed by 1913. The dam at Delta on the Mohawk River was built over the vehement protests of inhabitants who had to be relocated, but Hinckley folks on the West Canada Creek took the matter philosophically; they merely picked up their checks and settled elsewhere. Over the years, these two dams have been decided boons to the areas they serve. Herkimer, which was subject to severe annual floods, breathed more easily after the Hinckley dam was built. Both Hinckley Lake and Lake Delta provide recreational facilities for countless people each summer. These projects did not involve intrusion on the Adirondack Preserve, though the Blue Line has been extended to include part of the Hinckley reservoir.

The New York Board of Trade and Transportation, though not unaware of the need for water storage, stood firmly against any indiscriminate flooding of the Adirondack Park for the benefit of private power interests. A compromise was reached in 1913, when the Burd Amendment, permitting three per cent of the Forest Preserve to be flooded for water-storage purposes, was passed by two succeeding Legislatures and approved by the voters of the State, 486,264 to 187,290. Under this amendment, reservoirs were to be constructed by the State. The expense of improvements was to be apportioned on the public and private property benefited to the extent of benefits received.

The Conservation Department, headed by George D. Pratt, had its Division of Waters make a thorough study of the power and storage possibilities of the Black River and its tributaries between 1916 and 1918. Three engineers covered the whole Black River area, studied its topographical features, talked with industrialists who owned water rights along the rivers, proposed sites for reservoirs and estimated the cost of each. In 1919, the report of the engineers was published under the title, *Report on the Power and Storage Possibilities of the Black River*.

The engineers emphasized several factors: 1. Industries along the Black River owed their existence to water power and contributed much to the settlement and growth of Watertown and the villages along the Black River and its tributaries. 2. The ordinary spring freshet interfered with the operation of the mills between Carthage and Dexter and flooded the lowlands between Lyons Falls and Carthage for from 4 to 6 weeks each year, thus causing a large financial loss to property owners and others depending on the mills and the farm lands for their income. 3. Notwithstanding the regulating effect of the natural lakes, ponds and marshes and the existing reservoirs, the discharge was subject to such great fluctuations as to seriously impair the value of these streams for power production. "These low-water flows have made it impracticable under existing conditions to install power plants capable of utilizing more than a small percentage of the total flow of the stream and even within the economic limits of installation, the power output is of relatively low unit value due to the irregular and uncertain rate at which it may be produced. 4. It may be seen that the growth and prosperity of the community would be greatly enhanced by the construction of a system of storage reservoirs by which the flow of the principal streams would be controlled and regulated so as to furnish a more uniform output of water for manufacturing plants which in turn would profitably employ a largely increased number of operatives throughout the year."

Inasmuch as storage reservoirs close to plants using water power were preferable to distant points, and in view of the fact that industry along the Black River was concentrated between Carthage and Dexter, the engineers reported that a dam at Carthage would be the cheapest and most efficient to operate. The disadvantages outweighed the advantages: valuable farm land would be flooded; railroads and highways would have to be relocated; villages from Lyons Falls to Carthage would be inundated; water power on the upper stretches of the river would be seriously impaired. This Carthage reservoir, with a capacity of 64.5 billion cubic feet, would cost 12 million dollars to construct. The engineers, after considering all factors, reported that "a storage reservoir of any given capacity on this site is not commercially feasible for power purposes."

A proposed dam on the Black River a mile below Hawkinsville was also considered impractical. It would flood the river back to Forestport and force relocation of the village of Hawkinsville and, after the fight put up by the Delta inhabitants, this was a touchy subject. The six-mile lake would impound but 5.5 billion cubic feet of water, and the engineers did not feel that it would be worth the cost of construction.

The best site the engineers found on the Black River was at the dam which had created the Forestport Reservoir in 1894. It had several advantages: the land to be flooded was not valuable and it was outside the Blue Line; the chief extra cost would be the relocation of a portion of the Adirondack Division of the New York Central Railroad; four billion cubic feet could be added to the storage already available in existing reservoirs created for use by the canal system. The engineers came to the conclusion that, if the waters of the Moose and the Beaver could not be impounded, Forestport would be the next possible available site.

The Moose River possibilities underwent a thorough scrutinization. A dam at McKeever, backing up ten miles of the

Moose, and creating a reservoir with an available capacity of eight billion cubic feet of water, and involving land within the Blue Line but not owned by the State, was considered costly and infeasible, due to the fact that reservoirs further up the river could be built more inexpensively. Small reservoirs at Minnehaha, Nelson Lake and Indian Rapids were considered possibilities, though their combined capacities would be small. Enlargement of existing dams at Old Forge and Sixth Lake and a proposed new dam at Big Moose were ruled out, for the raising of water ten feet in the lakes would create difficulty in relocating camps and hotels along their shores.

On the south branch of the Moose, near Panther Mountain, the engineers discovered a site suitable for a reservoir with a maximum capacity of ten billion cubic feet. Six miles up from the end of the proposed Panther Mountain reservoir, they found, at Higley Mountain, another ideal site for a reservoir to impound 3.6 billion cubic feet of water. The land involved was entirely within the Blue Line: the 2,500 acres of forest land in the Panther Mountain area were all privately owned; of the 4,000 acres recommended for the Higley Mountain project, about 2,700 acres were owned by the State and the remainder by private interests. There were no villages to be moved, no railroads or highways to be relocated. The estimated costs of the dams were: Panther Mountain, $773,000 and Higley Mountain, $697,000. The engineers considered building of both dams highly feasible. The land, figured at $5 an acre, was cheap; the cost of construction was not high; the working head cost on the two reservoirs would be between 14 and 15 cents, as compared to 47 cents at Forestport Reservoir and 58 cents at Hawkinsville.

At the headwaters of the Beaver River, already utilized by four hydro-electric power plants, the engineers indicated three spots for dams: Lake Lila, the source of the river; Stillwater, where a reservoir had been built in 1882; a point one half mile below Eagle Falls. Small reservoirs on Otter Creek and Deer River were ruled out as impractical. By building a dam at Eagle Falls, improving the dam at Stillwater, and creating a reservoir at Lake Lila, the engineers reported that 3.6 billion cubic feet would be added to the present capacity of Stillwater at a cost of $779,800. These reservoirs, with a working head of 9.9 cents, would create the cheapest water power in the Black River system.

The report of the engineers reached this conclusion: "Under present conditions, owing to the extremely low stream flow during a part of the year, the total amount of energy available at the existing plants on the Black River watershed, which may be classified as 'Primary Power' (available continuously throughout the year) does not exceed 35,000 horsepower-years, while the total energy available at these plants within their respective installation is about 88,000 horsepower-years, showing that by far the larger part of the energy output of the present plants is secondary power.

"Under the conditions that would exist after the regulation of the flow of the Black, Moose and Beaver rivers, as hereinbefore described, and if the present plants were installed up to their economic limit, there would be available at these plants 113,000 horsepower-years of 'primary power' and in addition 39,000 horsepower-years of 'secondary power.'

"The ratio of the developed power to the undeveloped power is higher on the Black River than on any other of the principal streams in New York State, and if advantage is taken of the impounding basins that nature has placed in the watershed, there is no reason why the power resources of the Black River should not be fully developed."

XVII
RIVER CONTROL FAILS

DURING the boom years following World War I, the hydro-electric industry, represented in the North Country by the Northern New York Utilities, expanded by leaps and bounds. In their enthusiasm for developing electricity from water power, the companies played up the failure to utilize the "water now flowing idly to the sea" and emphasized the benefits the public would derive by permitting dams and reservoirs to be built, not only to control the flow of streams, but to bring added electric power to farms, villages and industry. They argued that hydro-electric plants were not ugly, that they were clean and noiseless in operation, that the high-tension lines were not unsightly and that transmission rights-of-way would prove useful as firebreaks and fire patrol lanes.

The State Legislature, enchanted by the boom which was sweeping the nation, followed the same line of thought. The Burd Amendment, ratified by the voters in 1913, had given the Legislature permission to make general laws to provide for the use of not exceeding three per centum of lands in the Forest Preserve "for the construction of reservoirs for municipal water supply, for the canals of the State and to regulate the flow of streams."

In 1915, the Legislature had passed the Machold Storage Law creating river regulating districts, which are State agencies with powers vested in a board of three persons appointed by the Governor for terms of three years. These districts are local organizations which confine their activities to their particular region of the State, and are formed after application from residents of that section.

The Black River Regulating District, with headquarters in Watertown, came into existence under the Machold Storage Law on May 7, 1919. Its members drew up a preliminary plan to enlarge the Stillwater Reservoir and to create twelve additional reservoirs capable of controlling 50 to 60 per cent of the flow of the Black River and its tributaries. Like the State engineers, the Black River Board discarded most sites as unfeasible and decided that the best possibilities for controlling the flow of the streams lay at Stillwater on the Beaver, Higley Mountain and Panther Mountain on the Moose and Hawkinsville on the Black. The ultimate decision was to enlarge the Stillwater Reservoir to a capacity of 4.72 billion cubic feet of water. The area to be inundated was 6,700 acres, including 3,092 acres within the Forest Preserve, or but ⅛ of one per cent of the three per centum permitted by the Burd Amendment. Though there was some opposition by conservationists, it was negligible, and the Black River Regulating District completed the dam at Stillwater in 1925. Though the Beaver contributes but nine per cent of the total flow of the Black at Carthage, the dam has mitigated the danger of flood and has provided regulation of flow on the Beaver, where several hydro-electrical plants and three paper companies run efficiently the year round. The flooding of the land involved no hardships to individuals and the lake is sightly.

The Burd Amendment included in its provisions the regulation of the flow of streams, and the Stillwater enlargement fell into that category. The lobbyists for the power companies and the legislators at Albany took what they considered a progressive step forward. In 1920, Senator Mortimer Y. Ferris of Ticonderoga submitted a resolution permitting the three per centum of the Forest Preserve allowed by the Burd Amendment to be used for "the development of water power and rights of way for electric transmission lines, all of which are hereby declared to be public uses." The resolution was passed by two Legislatures, as required by law, and submitted to the voters as a Constitutional amendment in 1923. While this resolution was still before the Legislature, that body passed, in 1921, the Water Power Act, which provided for the licensing of the State's water power sites to private individuals or corporations, who would be subject to public control and would pay annual rents for their rights.

Whereas the people of the State had known little about conservation when they had ratified the Burd Amendment in 1913, they had more definite ideas on the subject ten years later. The Conservation Department had embarked on a program of public education in 1919 with its first issue of *The Conservationist*. The Commission also kept conservation before the people through newspaper and magazine articles, lectures, slides and motion pictures. The Adirondack Mountain Club, later to be a prime factor in the Panther Mountain controversy, came into existence in 1922.

Though the power interests tried to lure the public with the siren song of public benefits, the voters had become disenchanted by promises made by electric companies. Citizens realized that benefits could be derived from electrical power, but they did not consider hydro-electric plants and transmission lines esthetic. Still rankling in the minds of many older people were the promises made by the Utica Gas & Electric Company when its dam was built at Trenton Falls on the West Canada Creek in 1901. To assuage fears that the famous falls would not be destroyed, the power company promised that it would not only preserve the beauty of the falls but would illuminate the chasm at night to add to the enjoyment of visitors. It did nothing of the sort, and Trenton Falls became merely a series of barren cliffs with a trickle of water falling over them.

In the Ferris Amendment, the idea of flood control and river regulation had given way to hydro-electric development in the Adirondacks, and the voters wanted no part of it. They sent it down to a resounding defeat, 965,777 to 470,251, and in that one stroke made it increasingly difficult for the Black River Regulating District in its later and futile efforts to control the Black River and its tributaries. The words "power grab" were to echo and re-echo through the years.

The Hudson River, subject to floods which often inundated streets in Albany and Troy, was brought under control through the construction of the Sacandaga Reservoir by the Hudson River Regulating District in 1930. This reservoir, like all projects sponsored by river regulating districts, was financed by assessments on downstream municipalities and private properties benefited by both flood control and low water improvement. Sacandaga Reservoir has been a success, for it enables industry to carry on during the summer months and prevents the use of rowboats on River Street in Troy and Broadway in Albany during spring floods. The lake has turned out to be a wonderful summer playground for the people of the State, and provides fishing through the ice in winter. The Conservation Department operates a public beach and camp site and boat-launching piers. Vacationists are enjoying the reservoir so much that they are at present engaged in a controversy with power interests and industries downstream, who do not wish to be deprived of water during the summer months merely to keep Sacandaga full for the enjoyment of summer vacationists. All of which goes to prove the old adage: "You can't please all the people all the time."

The Black River Regulating District watched the Sacandaga development with interest, and hoped to duplicate it in the upper stretches of the Moose River. The District was laboring under a severe handicap; the Sacandaga Reservoir had been located outside the Forest Preserve, whereas an impoundment of the Moose would involve flooding of land within the Blue Line.

During the depression years of the early Thirties, when money was being poured into the Public Works Administration's projects, the Black River Regulating District applied for Federal aid to build, at Panther Mountain, a reservoir capable of impounding 14 billion cubic feet of water. The people of the Black River valley needed such a reservoir but

Carthage Division of the Crown Zellerbach Corporation. Courtesy Crown Zellerbach.

Deferiet Division of the St. Regis Paper Co. Courtesy Niagara Mohawk Power Corporation.

Elmer Falls on the Beaver River, showing hydroelectric plant of Niagara Mohawk Power Corporation.

Sewall's Island, Watertown, showing Black Clawson and Niagara Mohawk Power Corporation plants.

could not finance it. The P. W. A. turned down the request, claiming that the money available to the Administration was not sufficient to undertake this project.

The trend was growing away from development of water power projects by private capital. The State entered the picture in 1930 by establishing the St. Lawrence Power Development Commission, which gave the State control of water power sites in the St. Lawrence region. A series of floods in the south-central part of the State in 1935 enlisted the interest of the Federal government. In the next year, Congress passed the Federal Flood Control Act, under which the Federal government assumed responsibility for flood control on navigable rivers and their tributaries. New York created the Flood Control Commission as a liaison agency with the Federal government. A happy relationship has existed between the State and Federal governments. Projects costing a total of 96 million dollars have been completed or projected since 1936, and the cost to the State has been less than a half million dollars.

As part of this long-range program, United States Army engineers conducted a survey of the Moose and Black Rivers. They submitted to the Speaker of the House of Representatives, on October 10, 1941, a recommendation favoring the construction of a multiple purpose reservoir of 14 billion cubic feet capacity at the Panther Mountain site. The estimated cost was $3,470,000 and the Black River Regulating District was willing to contribute $2,920,000 of this sum. Again, Federal aid was not forthcoming.

Inasmuch as the beneficiaries were not willing to pay for the entire cost of the Panther Mountain project, the Board submitted a proposal for a reservoir at Higley Mountain at a cost of $1,738,000. The Water Power and Control Commission gave the project its blessing, the Adirondack League Club raised no complaint except to state that it did not expect to pay any of the cost of the project, and an objection by Associated Properties was withdrawn in 1943. World War II brought a close to this hope of building a dam at Higley Mountain.

By 1945, the Black River Regulating District decided that the turn in events was going in its favor, for in the previous year Congress had approved the Panther reservoir as a Federal project. The Board resolved to provide without cost to the United States the necessary lands and easements, to maintain and operate the reservoir after its completion, and to hold the Federal government free from damage claims resulting from the construction of the reservoir. Local interests were to contribute the bulk of the cost of maintenance.

At this point, the conservationists took a hand in the proceedings. The Adirondack Mountain Club, Inc., a hiking and camping organization whose first aim was to preserve the "Forever Wild" amendment, held a conservation forum in Albany on October 21st. Over 100 representatives of more than 40 local, State and National organizations were in attendance. The first speaker called for immediate action to block the Panther Dam project and to devise some means of "sounding the tocsin" when similar threats to the Adirondacks arose in the future. A second speaker maintained that the flooding of the Moose River tract would obliterate "the best concentrated winter deer herding and feeding valley that we know today" and that the finest trout streams would be drowned out. He also pointed out that flood control in the dam project was of secondary consideration and that the chief purpose of the reservoirs, both Panther and Higley, was for the development of hydro-electric power. A resolution was passed to form a State-wide committee to attempt to halt "the proposed destruction of the Moose River valley." The Adirondack Moose River Committee was formed in February, 1946. Its object was "to preserve the wild forest character of the valley of the South Branch of the Moose River and other similar areas in the Adirondacks now threatened with destruction by the proposed creation of unnecessary reservoirs."

This resolution brought out a point of disagreement between the opposing forces. What the engineers, the Regulating District and the people of the Black River valley considered "necessary," became "unnecessary" to the Adirondack Moose River Committee and its backers, which included the Adirondack League Club, fish and game clubs, conservation councils and wild-life societies.

The Adirondack Moose River Committee let no grass grow under its feet. Within the space of a few months, it enlisted the support of more than 500 sportsmen's clubs, outing clubs and civic organizations, also such national conservation groups as the National Parks Association and the Fish and Wildlife Service. A pamphlet, *The Impending Tragedy of the Moose River*, was widely distributed, and motion pictures of the Moose River region were shown to clubs which requested them. Donations from interested parties were solicited. The theme of the Committee's propaganda was: Shall the largest remaining unspoiled primitive area in the Adirondacks remain a superb recreational region or shall it become a source of water power? Advocates of the "Forever Wild" principle were encouraged to send protests to Conservation Commissioner Perry B. Duryea, the Black River Regulating District and Governor Thomas E. Dewey. Duryea admitted that the volume of protests swamped his clerical force.

The conservationists had a stout champion in Leo Lawrence of Herkimer, chairman of the Legislative Assembly's Conservation Committee. Lawrence got a bill through the Assembly, blocking any further construction of reservoirs for power generation in the Forest Preserve by river regulating districts, but it was defeated in the Senate. In 1946, after the Black River Regulating District had failed to receive anticipated Federal funds and had decided to build the smaller Higley Mountain reservoir, Lawrence, insisting that the project was for hydro-electric development rather than for flood control, tried again and failed. At this point, Gov. Dewey emphasized that the Black River Regulating District should continue to build reservoirs in northern Herkimer County to provide better flood control and more hydro-electric power.

The Regulating District, taking this as a signal to go ahead, scrapped Higley and submitted plans for a reservoir at Panther Mountain with a storage capacity of not less than 12 billion cubic feet of water, and specified that nine billion would be for river regulation and three billion for flood control. Preliminary plans got the approval of the Water Power and Control Commission on May 4, 1948 and the Board ordered a public meeting, as required by law.

Seven sessions were held in Watertown between June 8th and July 9th. The River Regulating Board, which wanted to flood 3,190 acres of land owned or leased by the Adirondack League Club and 934 acres of State-owned land, argued that Panther Mountain was the most economical reservoir site on the Moose River outside of Higley Mountain; that it was the cheapest and most feasible, measured in terms of benefits, not only for flood control, but for pollution prevention and abatement, and for recreation. The Board had for its chief backers the Carthage Papermakers, the villages of Black River and Brownville, the town of Denmark, the Lewis County Board of Supervisors, the Lewis County Chamber of Commerce, the Lewis County Farm Bureau and the city of Watertown. Lined up against them were 36 organizations, including the Adirondack Mountain Club, the Adirondack League Club and the Adirondack Moose River Committee. They claimed that they were not against reservoirs as such, but were opposed to building a reservoir at Panther Mountain, claiming that it would result in the destruction of wild life and that it would take property unconstitutionally, under the guise of public use, for what was in reality private gain. They maintained that reservoirs at Port Leyden or Hawkinsville would better control the Black River. They sought a review of the Board's decision in the Supreme Court of New York, charging that production of hydro-electric power did not warrant destruction of natural forest cover, which was better for flood protection than reservoirs. Their arguments were not upheld by the Court.

"Forever Wild" advocates turned to the Legislature for help and got it. A Joint Legislative Committee on River Regulation was created in 1949 "to make a thorough study and investigation of the problem of existing and future river regulation within the state with a view to recommending appropriate legislation or constitutional amendments." In 1950, the Legislature passed and Gov. Dewey signed the Stokes Act, which stated: "No reservoirs for the regulation of the flow of streams or for any other purpose except for municipal water supply shall be hereafter constructed in Hamilton or Herkimer counties on the south branch of the Moose River by any river regulating board."

The Black River Regulating District challenged the constitutionality of the Stokes Act and met with a severe defeat. The Court ruled that the board of a regulating district had no right, as a creature of the Legislature, to challenge the constitutionality of a legislative act.

Regulation of the flow of the Black River and its tributaries, which had started out in 1919 as a regional project, had assumed State-wide importance by 1952, chiefly due to the unflagging efforts of the conservationist groups. A leading conservationist finally asked the question which had been expected for years: Why doesn't the River Regulating District have to answer to the poeple of the State for its operations?"

The Legislature was of the same opinion. Assemblyman John C. Ostrander of Saratoga County proposed an amendment to the Constitution which would strike out the words, "to regulate the flow of streams," from the Burd Amendment. The Ostrander Amendment was passed overwhelmingly in the Senate and the Assembly. Inasmuch as the resolution had to be passed by two Legislatures before the amendment came before the people, the Black River Regulating District hired a public-relations firm to promote its case before the Legislature and the public. It also got support from a few powerful organizations outside the North Country, including the State Grange and the State C. I. O. All efforts were to no avail: the 1953 vote in the Assembly was 122 to 29 and in the Senate 42 to 11 for the Ostrander resolution; the voters of the State approved the Ostrander Amendment by a vote of 943,200 to 593,696.

The Black River Regulating District tried again. The Wise-McGuiness resolution, seeking 1,500 acres in the Forest Preserve for a reservoir on the south branch of the Moose, was passed by two successive legislatures in 1954 and 1955. Once again, the decision was thrown into the laps of the voters.

The Battle of Panther Mountain, waged during the summer and autumn of 1955, involved two forces which were both advocates of conservation: the proponents of the dam and reservoir were interested in controlling the water resources of the Black River and its tributaries; the chief concern of the "Forever Wild" advocates was the preservation of the Adirondack forest lying within the area of the proposed reservoir.

Any citizen of the State who could read and who was at all interested in the proposed Wise-McGuiness Amendment could not have gone to the election booth poorly informed, for advocates of the opposing positions bombarded the electorate with pamphlets, and newspapers gave much space to the controversy, often taking editorial stands one way or the other.

The advocates of Panther Mountain reservoir argued:

1. Vast quantities of Adirondack water were going to waste, water that could be used to develop hydro-electric power on the Black River and its tributaries.

2. Lack of control in spring, resulting in inundation of land and flooding of factories, caused hardship and damage to people in the Black River valley.

3. The opposite effect, drouth in summer, created a danger of pollution and seriously hampered industry.

4. The cost of the project would be borne by the munici-

palities and industries in the region benefited and not by the tax-payers of the State.

5. The reservoir would add to the recreational enjoyment of all the people of the State.

6. The reservoir would use but 1,500 acres or .006 per cent of State land within the preserve and 3,100 acres from a private club which owned 100,000 acres within the Blue Line and would be paid for land condemned.

In rebuttal, the conservationists argued:

1. The Forest Preserve, the last primitive land in the Adirondacks, should be kept forever wild.

2. The Panther Dam project, though ostensibly for controlling the Moose River, was in reality one to benefit the hydro-electric industry.

3. Any concession would enable private interests to "put a foot in the door" and open up the Adirondacks to further exploitation.

The man in the street found the issues beclouded by two emotional factors: the conservationists played up the project as a "power grab" for the benefit of industrialists; the advocates of the reservoir berated the Adirondack League Club as "a group of wealthy men who had only their own interests at heart."

The voters of New York went to the polls on November 8, 1955 and defeated the Wise-McGuiness Amendment 1,-622,196 to 613,927. The amendment carried only in Lewis and Jefferson counties, the areas to be benefited by the construction of the reservoir.

The "Forever Wild" adherents won a smashing victory at the polls, but what may have been a gain for the people of the State has resulted in a serious loss for the people of the Black River valley. The Moose River still courses in its primitive way, carrying floods each spring which create "Lake Lewis" and threaten dams, bridges and mills along the Black River.

What can the now Hudson River–Black River Regulating

District do? Roscoe C. Martin, who presents a comprehensive study of the controversy in *Water for New York*, suggests three possibilities: the District might explore somewhat more carefully other reservoir sites; it might seek again to bring about repeal of the Stokes Act; it might try again to amend the Constitution to permit construction of storage reservoirs in the Forest Preserve. Martin admits that the third alternative seems unattainable and that the second would be extremely difficult. The only possibility, therefore, would be to control the Black River at Forestport, which would not prevent flooding or low water obstacles caused by the Moose or the sometimes rambunctious Sugar and Deer rivers.

Levi P. M. Gaylord of the Black River Regulating District, which lost the Battle of Panther Mountain, wrote in *Supervisors' News* for January, 1962: "From the studies being made by the Joint Legislative Committee on Natural Resources and the Temporary State Commission on Water Resources Planning, it is hoped that a new concept of water control and use will be born which will constitute true and honest conservation for the benefit of all the people of the State. It is becoming an urgent and serious problem and not one to be trifled with for pleasure or private gain."

XVIII
BUGLES AND DRUMS

THE BLARE of the bugle and the rattle of the drum have echoed throughout the North Country for a century and a half. Over the years, uniformed men have been familiar sights in villages from Carthage to Sackets Harbor.

Though the Treaty of Ghent in 1814 settled our differences with Great Britain, our government was not confident that a permanent end had come to hostilities, so Sackets Harbor was retained as a military base.

The Harbor had been an unhealthy place during the war. Smith's Cantonment, built to house 2,500 troops, had been overcrowded, dirty and ill-ventilated, with the result that about 1,400 soldiers and civilians had died of smallpox and other diseases.

Gen. Jacob Brown commissioned his brother, Maj. Samuel Brown, to erect, on the plateau where Old Sow had "grunted" at the British fleet in 1812, a series of stone buildings forming three sides of a square and open toward the lake. The stone was transported by water and hauled by ox-teams to the building site. Plaster was manufactured from lime burned in local kilns, and sand came from the beaches. Much of the labor was performed by soldiers assigned to the post. Madison Barracks, named after ex-President James Madison, were built between August, 1816 and October, 1819.

The stone buildings contained little in the way of comfort. The officers' quarters consisted of two downstairs rooms and an attic for sleeping. Buildings for the soldiers were each sub-divided into four equal rooms, with the rest of the space devoted to mess rooms, kitchens and storerooms. The men had no beds; they rolled up in blankets and slept on the floor. Heat was supplied by wood-burning fireplaces, while candles provided dim light. Water was brought up from the lake by prisoners. Each building had a privy behind it. Refuse was collected by prisoners and dumped into the forest outside the post. Grunting hogs wallowed in the mud and fought with skunks for this garbage.

The officer in charge during the building of Madison Barracks was Col. Hugh Brady of the Second Infantry, which consisted of five companies and about 600 men. Brady was a martinet who believed in severe punishment for misdemeanors—the ball and chain, whipping with the cat-o-nine-tails, gagging, shaving of heads, lashing to the wheels of cannon, beatings at dress parade, and even tarring and feathering. The people of Sackets Harbor, critical of the grog-shop activities of the soldiers and the tales of insubordination which emanated from Madison Barracks, dubbed the men, sarcastically, "Brady's Saints." The commandant was equal to the occasion. If his men were saints, he could prove it. One Sunday morning, he marched them to the Sackets Harbor meeting house, and continued to do so Sunday after Sunday for over ten years. His wife led a second procession of stylishly-dressed wives of officers.

President James Monroe visited the North Country in August, 1817. Escorted by Gen. Brown, he stopped at Ogdensburg, Antwerp, Le Raysville, Watertown and Brownville before reaching Sackets Harbor, where he inspected the post and reviewed Brady's regiment. He was entertained at the Mansion House by Bill Johnston, reputed to have been a British spy during the late war and later to gain further notoriety during the Patriot War. It is said that Johnston charged the President $150 for his brief stay at the Mansion House.

Three years later, Col. Brady removed the bodies of men killed in the Battle of Sackets Harbor, and the remains of Gen. Pike and others buried at Navy Point, and transferred them to a post cemetery within the stockade at Madison Barracks. This re-burial of the hero of the Battle of York, and subsequent exhumations and re-burials, started a controversy which may never end.

In 1831, William Morgan disappeared mysteriously while preparing a book purported to disclose the secrets of Free Masonry. Rumors arose that Morgan had been foully murdered after having been hidden in the Masonic Building in Sackets Harbor, and that one of the perpetrators of the crime had been the same Capt. King who had acted as Marshal of the Day during the reception to President Monroe.

The whole Black River country was thrown into a turmoil in 1837, when William Lyon Mackenzie of Toronto, who was in open rebellion against the Canadian government and, in particular, against the Governor-General, Sir Francis Bond Head, came to Watertown and established headquarters at the Mansion House in that village. Mackenzie's aim was to free the people of Canada from the patriarchal type of government led by Sir Francis Bond Head. American citizens along the border from Vermont to Detroit went a step further; they advocated Canadian independence and hinted at annexation to the United States.

Secret fraternities known as Hunters' Lodges spread like wildfire throughout the North Country. These lodges had a cloak-and-dagger appeal. Their initiation ceremonies, described fully by Oscar A. Kinchen in *The Rise and Fall of the Patriot Hunters*, were impressively frightening. As a penalty for breaking his oath, a man might have his throat cut to the bone, his house burned to the ground, and the remainder of his property destroyed.

Hunters' Lodges sprang up in Watertown, Cape Vincent, Clayton, Lowville, Sackets Harbor and other North Country villages. They appealed to reckless youths involved in the depression of the time; but, strange to relate, the leaders were often prominent men in their communities. Anthony Hood, a spy who gained entrance into lodge rooms in Watertown, Dexter and Sackets Harbor, "was surprised to see the respectability of the people who attended these lodges and the large amounts of money they subscribed and paid."

Watertown was the hot-bed of this revolt. At a mass meeting in the Public Square, 1,000 persons listened to inflammatory speeches and adopted a resolution declaring that the people of Canada should have immediate independence. At their headquarters in the Mansion House, Mackenzie, "Gen." John Ward Birge and "Commodore" Bill Johnston, laid plans for the several attempted invasions of Canadian soil.

The first move came in February, 1838. Gen. Rensselaer Van Rensselaer took an army of several hundred men to Clayton by sleigh. The Hunters had armed themselves by breaking into the arsenal at Watertown and stealing 400 stands of arms. The expedition, which had designs on Ganonoque and possibly Kingston, got as far as Hickory Island. Here Mackenzie threw a monkey wrench into the works by announcing that he did not want Van Rensselaer to lead the attack. News filtered through that the commandant at Kingston had gotten wind of the Patriot plans and was sending regulars to suppress the invaders. While Mackenzie was trying to enlist volunteers for his attack, a veteran of the War of 1812 added to the confusion by passing up and down among the half-frozen Patriots crying, "Before evening, you will all be massacred." The Patriots were not massacred. They beat a hasty retreat back to Clayton.

Mackenzie got a thrill one morning in late March, when hostlers dragged from the Mansion House stable his particular enemy, Sir Francis Bond Head. It seems that the British government, in order to ease the situation in Canada, had recalled the Governor-General. Bond Head had left Kingston secretly and had got to Watertown via Sackets Harbor. His plan was to take a stage to Rome, but his driver, either through confusion or by some premeditated plan, landed him at the Mansion House. The Governor-General, scared out of his wits, hid in the stable. According to legend, Mackenzie greeted him in a friendly manner, invited him to share breakfast, and put him on the morning stage for Rome.

The second move in the opéra-bouffe war came on the night of May 29th and 30th. Bill Johnston and twenty-two Patriots, painted like savages, boarded a British ship, the "Sir Robert Peel," at a wharf on Wells Island off Clayton, drove the passengers to shore in their night clothes, stole their money, and set the steamer afire. The victims spent an uncomfortable night huddled in a woodsman's shanty. In the morning, they were picked up by a British ship and taken to Kingston.

Johnston boasted that he was the leader of this outrage. Gov. William Marcy of New York hastened to Clayton and offered rewards for the capture of Johnston and other leaders. A much larger sum was put up by the Canadian government. Eight Canadians and one American were arrested and taken to the Watertown jail. Johnston was not among them.

Excerpts from the diary of Dyer Huntington indicated that Watertown was not solidly behind the Patriots. On February 24, 1838, he wrote: "Van Rensselaer and other straggling renegades from Canada are about our village since their ridiculous affairs at Clayton two days since. Several companies of militia are en route to protect the frontier." On March 28, he recorded: "Three days since the Governor of Upper Canada passed through our town on his way to England. To all appearances a small governor." And on June 5, Huntington told his diary: "The steamer Robert Peel was boarded last Wednesday morning while at a wharf on Wells Island below French Creek, plundered and burned. Some 12 or 15 of the perpetrators are here in jail awaiting the action of the grand jury. The governor is with us, and has issued a proclamation offering a reward for apprehensions." After the acquittal of the burners of the "Sir Robert Peel," Dyer commented: "Some rioting in the streets. Cannon fired by the patriots (or vagabonds) in honor of the liberation of their commander."

The commandant at Madison Barracks, Col. W. J. Worth, fitted out two steamers, the "Telegraph" and the "Oneida," both manned by members of his Eighth Infantry regiment. These vessels played hide and seek with Johnston's buccaneers all summer.

Despite this vigilance, Worth was unable to prevent an army of 400 Patriots from Northern New York from leaving the Harbor on November 11th on the steamer, "United States," for an attempt to take Prescott. The Gilbert and Sullivan cast now included Nils Szoltevsky Von Schoultz, a Polish refugee who possessed more idealism than Mackenzie and far more courage than Birge or Johnston. The expedition, after capturing two British ships and taking on more Patriots, reached Prescott without Birge, who had been taken ill and had returned to Ogdensburg for more volunteers, and Johnston, whose ship had gone aground.

Von Schoultz landed his men and fortified himself in a windmill. Heroically, but somewhat stupidly, he tried to defend his position against overwhelming odds. Birge and Johnston did not come to his aid, and the Canadians, who were supposed to rebel against their government, did nothing of the kind. Von Schoultz was forced to surrender. He and other leaders were tried and hanged; many other patriots were exiled to Van Dieman's Land, now Tasmania.

Col. Worth, with his two ships, lay off Wind Mill Point during the tragic stand of Von Schoultz. He could not interfere, even as an ally of the Canadians, for the battle was being fought on foreign soil.

Black River folks participated in this invasion. Among the prisoners were 17 from Watertown, 14 from the town of Lyme, 11 from Brownville and a scattering from other villages. Dorephus Abbey and Martin Woodruff of Watertown were hanged with Von Schoultz. Prisoners from Van Dieman's Land did not get back to the North Country until 1846. One of these men, Sylvanus S. Wright, was welcomed on his return with a street parade in the village of Copenhagen.

The saga of Bill Johnston did not end at the Windmill. He escaped the clutches of the Canadians, but was captured by United States law officers and taken to Auburn. He escaped again, was recaptured near Oneida Lake and was locked up in an Albany jail. While awaiting trial, he broke out again and disappeared among the Thousand Islands. The government evidently gave up on him, for he finished his career as keeper of Rock Island light, which shone on the spot where he had burned the "Sir Robert Peel."

Col. Worth and his Eighth Infantry worked wonders during their two year stay at Madison Barracks. Buildings and forts were repaired and painted, and a hospital, guard house, commissary and ordinance building were erected, all at a cost of $510,000.

Col. Worth greeted President Martin Van Buren in the summer of 1839. The Eighth Infantry was a snappy regiment. Gordon G. Heiner, Jr., in *From Saints to Red Legs*, gave this picture of the men on parade: "The men of the Eighth were a fine sight as they marched to the music of their band, with their long tailed coats drawn together by frogs across their chests, spotless white canvas trousers covering their black square toed boots, buttons gleaming like silver. Their long, unwieldy muskets reached to the shoulder without the bayonet point. When the latter was attached for parade, the 'long guns' were more than a foot higher than the soldiers' heads. Their caps were high and brilliant with decoration.

"The musicians were as gay as their favorite march, 'Yankee Doodle.' Bright red coats, cut straight around the bottom, were piped in yellow at the bottom and around the collar, and enormous brass epaulets shone upon their shoulders. They sported gold buttons, pale blue trousers, and high caps, topped with fur pompons and bearing their insignia, a gold bugle."

Col. Worth swelled with pride. At the close of maneuvers, he had his men load and fire a closing salvo toward the lake. One soldier wasn't too well-trained, for he forgot to remove the ramrod from his musket. The ramrod flew toward the sally port, where the President and the colonel were reviewing the regiment, and planted itself in the ground between the two celebrities.

Brownville and Watertown also got a look at "Little Van" during his tour. He had luncheon at the Brown mansion and was driven to Watertown, where he was greeted by ringing church bells and spontaneous cheers. He held a reception in the new American House and spent the night at the mansion of Micah Sterling.

Madison Barracks was sparsely populated from Sept. 22, 1840, when Col. Worth and his Eighth Infantry left to fight the Seminole War in Florida, until the close of the War with Mexico.

The Fourth Infantry moved in on November 13, 1848 and

with it came a 26-year-old West Pointer who had fought in the late war. First Lieutenant Ulysses Simpson Grant, who had been married less than three months, brought his bride with him to Madison Barracks.

The Grants lived on post that winter, left for Detroit for two years, returned in June, 1851 and departed the following year. Grant served as quartermaster of the regiment, and was remembered by Harbor folks as a quiet little man who loved horses and hated band music, though he was in charge of the band. Grant wore his hair long but shaved his beard. He was addicted to smoking cigars and chewing tobacco, but he abstained from liquor and helped to start a chapter of the Sons of Temperance at the Barracks. He disliked dances and social affairs, but loved to play poker and checkers. He would dash off to Watertown on horseback to play checkers with the champion of that village, making the ten miles in 45 minutes. On one occasion, when he had played one of his innumerable draws with his Watertown opponent, who was an old shoemaker, they decided to settle the issue with a foot race, which the young lieutenant won going away.

At the opening of the Civil War in 1861, Madison Barracks was practically abandoned and the buildings had become badly run down. Four volunteer regiments were mobilized and got their first training there, the Ninety-Fourth Infantry in 1861, the Tenth Artillery in 1862, the Twentieth Cavalry in 1863 and the 186th Infantry in 1864. Sackets Harbor became a refuge for deserters from the British army who came across the lake and took bounties to enlist in Federal regiments. It also was a gathering place for men seeking substitutes to avoid the draft. Sums up to $1500 were paid for Canadian substitutes.

The years of negligence and the training of war regiments practically ruined Madison Barracks, and a severe fire in 1876 levelled a large section of the officers' quarters. Gen. William Tecumseh Sherman wished to abandon the post and opposed efforts to rebuild the burned sections. The garrison, around

Madison Barracks, Sackets Harbor. Stone Row in 1945, when post was abandoned. *Watertown Daily Times.*

Camp Drum, the training ground for national guardsmen near Great Bend. *Watertown Daily Times.*

Industry Has Left Glen Park. This "Roman ruin" is the flume of the abandoned Remington Paper Co. *Watertown Daily Times.*

But the Black River Rushes on. Early spring at Glen Park, showing power of the river. *Watertown Daily Times.*

1880, consisted of five or six men. Madison Barracks seemed doomed as a military post.

Somebody must have had a change of heart, for Gen. Orlando B. Wilcox arrived on Sept. 12, 1882 with six companies from the Twelfth Infantry. Wilcox improved the buildings, installed partial sewers and built a high water tank to provide better drinking water and protection from fire. Gen. Sherman came on a tour of inspection and was impressed with what Wilcox had done.

Madison Barracks assumed the appearance known to the present generation under Col. Charles C. Barrett, who came to the Harbor with his Ninth Infantry in 1891 and stayed 14 years. He remodelled the old stone buildings, built new brick officers' quarters and barracks for soldiers, and put up a brick mess building. Succeeding officers beautified the grounds by transplanting maple trees from the surrounding woods to the post land and by planting hundreds of lilac bushes. An athletic field was laid out and post teams were organized to compete against outside aggregations. In winter, officers raced ice boats on the lake. A Negro regiment won its way into the hearts of Sackets Harbor residents with its snappy band. And, in 1913, a future President, Franklin Delano Roosevelt, spoke at the 100th anniversary of the Battle of Sackets Harbor.

During World War I, Madison Barracks served as a training camp for officers, and at one time 2,500 men were stationed there. Near the close of the war, the Barracks became General Hospital No. 37. The Barracks also served as a receiving center for French war brides, who added to the coffers of local movie houses and stores with their total disregard for the value of money.

Madison Barracks got its first artillery regiment in September, 1922. The change to artillery meant the building of barns for horses and sheds for cannon. This artillery outfit, the Seventh Field Artillery, would drill and parade at the drop of a hat, and Watertown and smaller places were often benefited by their appearances. Madison Barracks also trained men in the Citizens Military Corps. The R. O. T. C. sent men from Cornell and Princeton each summer. The Army Olympic tryouts for horsemanship were held at the post in 1922, and polo games between army teams provided Sunday afternoon entertainment for the soldiers and the villagers.

When the Twenty-Eighth Infantry joined the artillery in 1926, several new buildings were erected, including large brick barracks with slate roofs, three brick apartment buildings, a new administration building, a fire house and a riding hall. Movies and entertainments were held in Dodge Hall, the abandoned administration building. After it burned to the ground in 1932, a brick theater was built.

Abandonment of Madison Barracks had been talked about since the Civil War days. During the first administration of President F. D. Roosevelt, the outcry rose again, but the post remained, though it became increasingly difficult for the officers to obtain needed articles.

The artillery at Madison Barracks became mechanized in 1934, when the Seventh Field Artillery became the Second Battalion of the Twenty-Fifth Field Artillery. The "passing of the horse" raised a terrific controversy. Men of the Seventh, cherishing tradition, did not want to lose its horses. People in Sackets Harbor and nearby villages protested vehemently when horses were transferred, sold or destroyed.

The arrival of mechanized artillery at Madison Barracks altered the character of the frontier post. The rifle range at Stony Point near Henderson Harbor, in use since 1895, was transferred to the jurisdiction of Fort Ontario. Madison Barracks, with its 100 acres of land, became unsuitable for large-scale artillery maneuvers, and much of this activity was transferred to Pine Plains near Great Bend.

Pine Plains, embracing the James Le Ray de Chaumont residence and later the lumbering area for Felt's Mills, became an experimental training site in 1908. The United States Army leased 10,000 acres from the Watertown Chamber of Commerce and held an encampment that summer for regular troops and National Guardsmen from New York, New Jersey, Pennsylvania and several New England states. Almost ten thousand troops, quartered in tents, participated in sham battles and other maneuvers, with cavalry as a mobile element. The maneuvers were so successful that the Army purchased the land the following year.

Pine Camp became the scene of annual maneuvers, the largest of which took place in August, 1935. The motorized Twenty-Fifth Artillery from Madison Barracks came early and stayed late, and provided transportation to the camp for the 36,500 troops who arrived in Watertown by railroad. The Post Hospital at the Barracks became the base hospital for the First Army, which participated in sham battles at Pine Camp, along with National Guard units from the New England states, the Twenty-Seventh New York and the Forty-Fourth New Jersey. This extensive military exercise, designed to test mobilization and supply, was highly successful.

In 1939 and 1940, the War Department purchased another 90,000 acres at Pine Camp and began the construction of buildings to accommodate 20,000 troops. Pine Camp was active during World War II and continued on a permanent basis until 1953, when it became a summer training ground for National Guard units.

The story of Madison Barracks after the war is one of continual frustration for the people of the North Country. The post was deactivated and the barracks were declared surplus by the Army in November, 1945. Here were some 174 buildings, chiefly built of stone and brick, located on 100 acres of ground overlooking Lake Ontario, constituting a village within itself, with water supply, electric power, mess hall, theater, drill shed, administration building, and housing facilities for at least 1,000 people.

The village of Sackets Harbor, deeply concerned over the abandonment of Madison Barracks, tried all ways possible to keep some kind of installation there. A training base for the

United States Navy and a proposed site for the new United Nations were both turned down. St. Lawrence University, Ithaca College and St. John's College of Annapolis, Maryland all sent representatives to inspect the Barracks, but none chose to use them for educational purposes. In 1950, a proposed foreign service academy received scant attention. Suggestions for use of the Barracks as a soldiers' home or a mental-hygiene hospital made little impression. Sackets Harbor tried to get the new Air Force Academy in 1950 and Champlain College two years later. Its efforts brought no results.

The death blow to Madison Barracks came in 1954, when the War Assets Administration put the property up for sale through sealed bids by private individuals or corporations. The first bids were refused as too low, but the Barracks finally went to the Pariser Enterprises of Long Branch, N.Y. in 1955 for $226,000. The story since that date is one of hopeless confusion, involving new owners, mortgages and tax delinquencies.

Pine Camp was officially named Camp Drum on December 3, 1951 in honor of Lt. Gen. Hugh A. Drum, a First Army Commander during the early years of World War II. Pine Camp, in 1948, and Camp Drum, in 1952, conducted winter maneuvers known respectively as "Snowdrop" and "Snow Fall." The people of the Black River valley took these parachute operations to heart, feeling alternate concern for the men who were dropped from airplanes into the snow-covered wilderness around High Market and a certain pride that their area had been chosen for this exercise.

Camp Drum, since 1953, has become chiefly a summer operation for the training of National Guard units from New England, New York and New Jersey. The exercise is conducted in seven two-week training periods from early June until September. Between 75,000 and 90,000 reservists come to Camp Drum each summer in installments of from 7,000 to 13,000 men. For example, the 1963 exercise will start June 8th with 8,500 men from the Massachusetts 26th Infantry and will close on August 31st, when New York's 8,000-man 42nd Infantry Division completes its fortnight of training.

Camp Drum, built chiefly of wood, contains over 1,000 buildings, including barracks, churches, theaters, bowling alleys, a library and athletic fields. Several Post Exchanges cater to the needs of soldiers. Overall administration is carried on by 3,000 officers and men of the United States Army, who arrive in late April and remain until October. They rehabilitate and maintain ranges, improve facilities and housing areas, and provide logistical, financial and administrational support for the operation.

The first week consists of individual training, including marksmanship, drills, classes and arms qualification. The second week offers added instruction and certain larger unit exercises. The 108,000 acres at Camp Drum include ample facilities for combat exercises, including a vast artillery range.

The Black River valley, which witnessed the passing of troops to and from Sackets Harbor during the War of 1812, is traversed by army convoys every second weekend from June to September. Long lines of jeeps and trucks, interspersed with special vehicles, wend their way along the highways in the midst of weekend traffic. These convoys have become better regulated within recent years, being broken up into smaller units and controlled by military police at important road intersections. The coming and going of these well-uniformed National Guard units is a far cry from the bedraggled troops who raided orchards and hen-roosts during the War of 1812.

The annual influx of 75,000 to 90,000 soldiers each summer makes a striking impact on the economy of the North Country and also creates problems of military-citizen relationships. Each unit is free on its first weekend at Camp Drum. The soldiers, most of whom are young, spend freely in Watertown and other communities. The Watertown Chamber of Commerce estimates that about three million dollars are put into circulation each summer by soldiers on leave. The authorities at Camp Drum try to encourage the men to visit points of interest in the North Country. People in Watertown and other communities often invite soldiers as weekend guests. A National Defense Committee, composed of officers and civic leaders, fosters good relationships between the two groups. Two Open House days are held each summer, when civilians of the area come to Camp Drum to witness parades and military demonstrations. Officers at Camp Drum make efforts to orient the soldiers on standards of conduct during off-duty time. The results are for the most part good, though there are the usual dislocations concomitant with soldiers on leave.

Camp Drum is situated on what was once the vast estate of James Le Ray de Chaumont. The limestone mansion where James Le Ray lived still stands on the outskirts of the military encampment. It is set against a backdrop of trees and is surrounded by spacious lawns, and may look much as it did in 1827. It forms a connecting link between the past and the present at Camp Drum.

XIX
A RIVER RAMBLE

THE UPPER STRETCHES of the Black River have reverted to nature. Two roads wind their way through the forest and past a few houses and camps from Forestport to North Lake. The old road, which Tom O'Donnell dwelt upon lovingly in *The Birth of a River*, still leaves Buffalo Head (Forestport Station) and crosses the Black River at Enos, where Tom's friend and mine, Dell Bellinger, used to sit on his ramshackle porch and feed peanuts to his pet chipmunk, Teaser. It turns left at Goldie Roberts' place and wanders through the woods on a dirt trail which has seen little improvement over the years.

The Farrs and the Bronsons are gone, as are the Reeds at Reed's Mill, where the road crosses the river again to meet the newer road from Buffalo Head. The only thing different about the second road is its hard surface and a treacherous hill descending to Reed's Mill, where it joins the older road to North Lake, South Lake and Honnedaga (Jock's) Lake. Glamor of a sort has been added by the air force tower, a sky-piercing spire of steel set on a gigantic ball. Louse Hill has been dignified by the name, St. Leger Hill, though that British officer never came within thirty miles of the spot.

The State dam at North Lake still releases a stream of coffee-colored water which rushes madly toward the sea. Fishermen have taken over where small lumber mills once stood, and the river is stocked annually with trout. A deer darts through the woods on occasion, and bristly porcupines are sometimes encountered along the needle-strewn paths. Otherwise, all is the silence of the forest and the music of the stream.

The shores of artificial Kayuta Lake (Forestport Reservoir) are dotted with camps, and fishermen can be seen dangling lines from Ebert's Bridge and Dustin's Bridge in the hope of catching bass or perch. The lake offers problems for the campers. When filled, it is an attractive sheet of water, but, during some summers, the water gets so low that Kayuta is merely a collection of stumps surrounded by mud and a trickle of water.

The lumbering activities at Woodhull and Forestport vanished years ago. Forestport, with no important industry, lives the life of a small village, with its stores, hotels and churches catering to the permanent population and putting on a show of importance to impress summer campers. Water spills over the dam and the natural falls below, and the Black River canal feeder wends its way beside the river toward Boonville.

The river at Hawkinsville is a thrilling sight as it cascades under the bridge. The village would be but a small edition of Forestport if it were not for the thriving Brant Excelsior

Company, built on the site of the old Anderson Bros. tannery. Walter Brant, in 1910, bought an excelsior mill which had been built beside the river by D. C. West of Lowville ten years earlier. For over fifty years, the Brant Excelsior Company, using local basswood and poplar, has been making excelsior for use in the manufacture of glue, for stuffing toys and foot-stools, and for drug-store packings. The plant is of special interest, for its 100 horse power wheel is turned by water from the Black River. Brant retired in 1951 and sold the mill to the present operators, Mr. and Mrs. Stanley Presta.

The Sugar River quarry, which supplied stone for the locks of the Black River Canal, was opened up in 1963 as the Boonville quarry by The S. DeLia Corporation of New Hartford, which is crushing the limestone for use in building roads. J. Talarico, Inc. of Mohawk has a blacktop plant at the same location.

The Boonville Electric Light and Power Company, since 1903, has operated a plant at Denley, below where the Sugar River enters the Black. The company not only furnishes light and power for the village of Boonville, but also serves parts of seven townships. In 1958, it entered into a contract with the Power Authority of the State of New York and at the present time 25% of the power is generated at Denley and 75% comes from the Seaway. The arrangement has been successful, for the company has reduced rates four times since 1958 and has no indebtedness. The company is municipally owned and is controlled by a board of commissioners appointed by the village board.

The highway passes through Port Leyden along the route of the abandoned Black River Canal. A large sign at the southern entrance to the village attempts to lure investors by boasting of Port Leyden's water power and factory sites, but the only two industries on the river are a small sawmill and a hydro-electric plant. The site of the Snyder Bros. tannery is occupied by the Port Leyden Central School. Crumbling vestiges of the "iron experiment" can be seen farther down the river.

Port Leyden saw a ray of hope in 1948, when the Kelly-Forsythe Company purchased the abandoned Gould paper mill, remodelled it, and began to make some of the finest tissue paper in the world. The company also built, on the ruins of the Johnston & Son pulp mill, which had burned in 1945, a hydro-electric plant. Kelly-Forsythe carried on for six years, turning out fine paper and giving employment to men of Port Leyden. The firm evidently over-stepped itself, for it went bankrupt in 1954. The mill is now operated as a small sawmill by Roderick Loomis; and Raymond Bailey, at the hydro-electric plant, sells his power to the Niagara Mohawk Power Corporation. Otherwise, the excellent water power is wasted.

The "grand old man" of Port Leyden is John E. Johnston who, in addition to running the family pulp mill, also became one of the biggest lumber contractors in the Black River area. Space does not permit a description of the many lumbering activities engaged in by Mr. Johnston since 1916. Let it suffice to say that he lumbered at Brantingham, on Tug Hill, at Tupper Lake, South Lake, Jerseyfield Lake and Long Lake, also along the West Canada Creek at Nobleboro.

The significant thing about Mr. Johnston is that he represents the present-day scientific school of logging, one that is conscious of the value of forests and responsive to innovations. For example, he introduced the method of building roads up to the log piles in the woods, so that trucks could haul the logs to market. He was one of the first to bring tractors into the woods. He also was a pioneer in the introduction of the chain saw and the bull-dozer. He installed shops in his camps, so that repairs of equipment could be made at the scene of operations. At the time of his retirement in 1959, he had supervised, over 43 years, the cutting and transportation of about 900,000 cords of pulp wood and 60,000,-000 feet of lumber products, chiefly hardwood.

The present village of Lyons Falls is a far cry from the cluster of huts built near the foot of the High Falls by an impractical group of French aristocrats almost 170 years ago. It also has little in common with the days of the Black River Canal, for few vestiges of that engineering achievement remain in the village.

Lyons Falls, for most of its life as a village, has been under the paternal care of the Lyon and Gould families, with an assist from the Merriams. Caleb Lyon, the patriarch, owned most of the land along the Black and Moose rivers, and his family controlled the water power at Lyonsdale and Lyons Falls. G. H. P. Gould, the lumber baron, developed the pulp and paper industry. The Gould Paper Company has been the backbone of the village for over a half century, for it has created employment and contributed in many other ways to the development of the community.

The Gould family passed out of the picture in 1945, when Gordon H. P. Gould, grandson of the founder of the Gould Paper Company, sold out to the Continental Can Company, though the name of the firm was not changed. Continental Can revamped the screen room and the wood room and built an office building, a steam plant, a finishing room, and a ground-wood bleach plant.

Continental Can sold the mill to the International Basic Economy Corporation of New York in 1951. This company, headed by Nelson A. Rockefeller, made the transaction in association with Cia. T. Janer Comerco E. Industria of Rio de Janeiro, Brazil. IBEC entered into a long-term contract to provide paper for Brazil. Ralph W. Leuthi, a veteran paper maker, became president. An acute shortage of spruce for pulp wood arose. The sulphite mill was shut down, and sulphite and kraft were brought in from outside. The discovery that hardwood could be used to manufacture wood pulp caused IBEC to put up a hardwood plant to conserve spruce.

In 1956, the Lyons Falls Paper Corporation, headed by Leuthi, bought the Gould plant and continued operation as the Gould Paper Company. Last year, the mill was sold again, this time to the Puget Sound Pulp and Timber Company. In April, 1963, this firm consolidated with Georgia-Pacific.

The Gould Paper Company, as of the present, is manufacturing a book grade paper suitable for high-class magazines. If you read *Christian Herald, Modern Needlework, True, True Story, T V Guide* or *Woman's Day*, chances are that you will be holding in your hands the product of Lyons Falls' leading industry.

Far up the Moose River, McKeever carried on in various forms an industry which dates back many years, when the Moose River Lumber Company operated at that place. The Rice Veneer Company took over and manufactured fine veneer from birch logs from lands owned by the Gould Paper Company. Georgia-Pacific bought the Rice plant and added a matching plant, where veneer was cut up, matched, and made into beautiful panels, which were shipped to markets in the South and West. A few years ago, Georgia-Pacific moved out and sold the plant and the village of McKeever at auction. Moyer & Pratt, Inc., which had operated under that name at Lyonsdale for over 60 years, sold out on Jan. 1st of this year to Colin Gardner. As Cogar, Inc., this firm is expanding operations at Lyonsdale and will manufacture jumbo rolls to sell to converters, and possibly tissue paper and napkins.

To reach the Cogar plant, the famous three-way bridge must be crossed. Take a good look at strangers in cars before you use the time-worn gag, "Go to the middle of the bridge and turn left." A Lyons Falls wag said just that last summer and was shocked when the motorist reached out of the car window and punched him in the nose. The native felt better when the motorist, after crossing the bridge, turned around and came back to apologize.

If you have never seen this "Y" or three-way bridge, do so right away, for a movement is on foot to replace it with two bridges, one across the Black, the other across the Moose. Sentiment favors retaining the landmark, but trucks hauling logs to the Gould mill can't get across the old bridge and have to take an expensive roundabout route to Lyons Falls. Experience has taught us that utility usually conquers sentiment.

A left turn leads to Greig and passes the imposing mansions of the descendants of the Lyon family. Walter D. Edmonds' novel, *The Big Barn*, gives a fictional account of the building of a barn on the Lyon estate. The benefactors of Lyons Falls could not have chosen a more attractive site, overlooking the Moose as it joins the Black and the thrilling High Falls of the main river.

The Black River becomes placid as it reaches Greig, a neat, tiny hamlet dozing quietly beside the stream, with a spur road leading to Brantingham Lake, a popular summer resort for campers and the site of a boys' camp. Deerlick Rock still stands like a sentinel guarding the river.

Until the Black River & Utica Railroad came through in 1869, Glenfield consisted of a dozen houses, a mill, a store, a church, and locks at the mouth of Otter Creek through which canal boats and steamers passed en route from Lyons Falls to Carthage. The first settlement was at Glensdale on Whetstone Creek, nearly a mile back from the river, and it was at this location that early gristmills and sawmills operated. The railroad and the canal brought about a shift of population to the village on the Black River, which was first Glendale and later Glenfield.

The new village was a busy place. Five sawmills were in operation on Otter Creek and tanneries brought in hides from Argentina for tanning into leather. Glenfield was also a fueling station for the railroad and great quantities of rock maple were cut on Tug Hill and piled near the Glenfield station for use by the wood-burning locomotives. Lafayette Wetmore built a table factory near the station. The original building, with additions, is now occupied by a subsidiary of the Beaverite Corporation of Beaver Falls. It is Glenfield's only industry.

Back in 1927, the Quinn brothers, Martin and Evan, came over from Olean, built a huge wooden factory between the Wetmore mill and the river, and started to manufacture alcohol, acetate, ether, dyestuffs and charcoal. To secure wood for this ambitious operation, they took over the log railroad G. H. P. Gould had built years before to carry logs to the canal. This railroad, the Glenfield and Western, ran from Glenfield to Page, high in the Tug Hill region. Other branch lines were started toward No. 4 in the Independence River country.

This Keystone Chemical Company was one of the wonders of the Black River valley. The capital investment, supplied by the Quinns and local investors, was very large. The factory ran at full tilt for about two years, and Glenfield envisioned itself as the manufacturing center of the area. Storekeepers, bankers and other suppliers of Keystone, confident that success was just around the corner, extended credit to the Quinns beyond normal limits. The bubble burst in the spring of 1929, when the Keystone Chemical Company went bankrupt. The mill closed and the network of railroads was abandoned. To add to the desolation caused by this failure of a promising industry, Glenfield, in August of the same year, was nearly wiped off the face of the map by a disastrous fire which took a hotel, several homes and the store of the man who had extended too much credit to the Keystone Chemical Company.

It has taken Glenfield years to recover from these blows, but the village seems to have become reconciled to living the life of the small place it was before the Keystone fiasco. The General Martin Central School—now part of the Southern Lewis system—serves as an attractive entrance to the village from the Lyons Falls to Lowville highway. The stores, hotel and houses are well kept up. The abandoned railroad station has been converted into a shop. The Beaverite Corporation offers employment and an industrial atmosphere. And, finally, the village has been promised a new bridge across the Black

River, not at the present location, but on the site of the second Tiffany Bridge.

Below Glenfield, the Black River is joined by Otter Creek and the Independence River, streams highly important during the lumbering era but not used by industry today. The electric plant on Otter Creek has been abandoned, and nothing is left of Dannatsburg on the Independence. Watson, one of the earliest settlements, has never realized the hopes of its eccentric founder. The church which Tom O'Donnell described in *The River Rolls on* still stands proudly by the wayside. Beach's Bridge, the oldest span crossing the Black River, is being replaced by a new and larger structure.

Beach's Bridge has for years been the focal point for information on the annual spring floods which create the infamous "Lake Lewis." Folks travelling from Glenfield to Lowville via Watson in early spring always ask, "Is Beach's Bridge open?" before undertaking the trip. They hope the answer is "Yes," for Watson is probably the most isolated community in the North Country during the month of April.

Lowville, the county seat of Lewis County since 1864, shows evidence of being proud of its status. Though it has a population of less than 4,000, the village gives the impression of being a larger place. State Street, the main thoroughfare, is wide and spacious, indicative of the foresight used by the pioneers in laying out the village. The entrance from the south is impressive, with the 133-year-old stone Presbyterian Church serving as a terminus to the long street and lending, with its white spire, a touch of the New England from which the founders of the village came. The Lewis County Courthouse, restored after a bad fire some years ago, maintains in its pillared façade the dignity which coincides with justice.

In the beginning, the courthouse and the academy were one. Things have not changed appreciably, for the Lowville Academy and Central School stands shoulder to shoulder with the present seat of county government. The school is a far cry from the old Lowville Academy, and some of the older folks in the village must shudder at the modernistic additions which have been made to it. Attractive they are, but somewhat out of keeping with the conservative aspect of the village.

Lowville's background has always been agricultural. The early settlers came because they were impressed by the rich farm lands stretching from the Black River toward Tug Hill. Today, extensive farms bespeak of the agricultural resources which have made and maintained Lowville. Farm organizations abound: the Lewis County Farm Bureau, started on a small scale in 1912, has over 1,300 members; the Lewis County Home Bureau, organized in 1920, brought farm women into the picture. Over the years, the Farm Bureau and the Home Bureau have worked through county agents and home demonstration leaders to improve methods of farming, to bring new ideas into home-making and to carry on projects designed to improve conditions on the farms and in the community. An important project was the inauguration of 4-H clubs for the young people, thus encouraging the future generation to take a definite interest in scientific farming and forest conservation.

Two pillars of Lowville's agricultural life antedate these organizations. Lowville Grange No. 71 was organized on February 4, 1874. Its growth was slow, and it was not until the Grange obtained its own building in 1912 that it became a potent force in the community. The Grange has agitated for better roads, rural free delivery and the teaching of agriculture in the schools. It was also behind the formation of the Farm Bureau and the Home Bureau.

The Lewis County Agricultural Society, formed in 1841, held annual fairs in Denmark, Constableville, Lowville, Turin and West Martinsburg until 1871, when it established itself at the county seat. Five years later, the Society bought Forest Park and built the present fair ground at that spot.

The Lewis County Fair has retained most of the features of the old New England fairs. Though its opening parade is

spectacular, with its marching firemen and its prancing major-
ettes, the fair is not merely one more carnival, but features
exhibits devoted to agriculture. Though the wooden buildings
are old, the grounds are spacious, and what remains of Forest
Park provides shade where families can hold reunions and
farmers can complain about the milk situation.

Lowville reflects the business changes which have come to
all villages over the past fifty years. Carriage-makers and other
artisans who catered to the horse have given way to automobile dealers, garages and filling stations. The railroad which
the villagers greeted with joy a century ago no longer offers
passenger service. Chain stores have to some extent replaced
local merchants in dispensing dry goods and food. Professional services have not increased in proportion to the growth
of the village.

The national trend toward centralization has affected the
dairy industry. Milk is no longer marketed by individuals,
but is brought to the Lowville Producers Dairy Co-operative,
Inc. Lewis County still occupies a prominent position in
cheese manufacture, but the small factories which dotted the
countryside have disappeared one by one, and the bulk of
cheese-making in Lowville takes place at the Kraft Foods
Division of the National Dairy Products Corporation, where
American cheese in bulk is made from milk purchased from
the co-operative. Farmers buy most of their feed from the
Lowville Farmers' Co-operative, Inc., which also operates
an extensive hardware store. And, though the Lewis County
Trust Company still operates independently, the Black River
Bank has become part of the system of the Watertown Na-
tional Bank, and occupies an attractive new building on State
Street.

The Kellogg House, once the pride of Lowville, has been
the Hotel Bateman for over a half century, chiefly under the
direction of a member of the Mahar family. Harold J. Mahar
and his wife are presently in charge. The Bateman has aged
gracefully. No attempt has been made to "modernize" the

hotel. The lobby floor of "pure marble" has withstood the tread of thousands of boots, and the dining room has a Victorian air which no modern hotel could duplicate.

Lowville, which merely dabbled in industry in the past, has acquired two enterprising firms. Payne-Jones, Inc., started in 1935, employs 100 people in coating paper by a chemical process and embossing it. This specially-treated paper is converted from Latex, Kraft and other substances, and is shipped in rolls to manufacturers of book and catalog covers. The United Block Company, which built a plant at Croghan in 1917 for the purpose of manufacturing shoe lasts, has developed into one of America's leading makers of bowling pins. In 1957, the American Machine & Foundry Co. of New York, built a plant in Lowville for finishing bowling pins. The Croghan plant was utilized to make rough blocks until it burned in January, 1960. Blocks are now made at a mill in Lowville and finished at the United Block Company, which is a division of the New York firm. "Chemwood" bowling pins are turned out at the rate of two million a year, and the company gives employment to 270 people.

Though changes have come to Lowville, it still retains the appearance of a New England village, with its immaculate streets, attractive churches and carefully-tended houses and lawns.

It is not always possible to take the road from Lowville which crosses the Black River at the Illingworth Bridge, for that area is part of "Lake Lewis" during April. Though the land is flooded annually, and commuters must take roundabout routes to places of business, the farmers take the proceeding as a matter of course, for they have lived with these floods all of their lives and hold no hope that the condition will be corrected. They grow, near the river, a coarse-grained variety of hay which yields profusely.

The tree nursery of the State Division of Lands and Forests at Dadville suffers inconvenience from flooding, mainly because the water gets into the seed beds. This nursery, established in 1922, raises from 40 to 50 million conifer seedlings each year. These seedlings are raised for State and private reforestation and can be purchased by citizens at $10 per 1000 seedlings.

The "pretty Beaver River," so described by a pioneer at what was to have been the French capital, Castorville, has lost none of its attractiveness. Unlike the rampaging Moose, it is a dignified stream, controlled effectively by the Stillwater Reservoir. Much of the electricity for the Black River country is generated from water power supplied by the Beaver. The J. P. Lewis Company operates plants at High Falls and at Beaver Falls. The Niagara-Mohawk Power Corporation uses water power from the river at seven locations. These plants—Belfort, Taylorville, Elmer Falls, Effley Falls, Soft Maple, Eagle Falls and Moshier—have a combined rated capacity of 39,810 kilowatts.

Manufacturing on the Beaver River is chiefly concentrated at Beaver Falls, where three thriving firms give employment to 450 to 500 people from the surrounding area. The J. P. Lewis Company which specialized for years in a wall board known as "Beaver Board," is at present specializing in pulp and sulphite cover paper, specialty board and bottle top board. The company has installed a modern electric pulp-grinder, but brings in sulphide from outside. The old Lewis, Slocum and Le Fever mill is occupied by the Latex Fiber Industries, a subsidiary of the United States Rubber Co. At Beaver Falls, this company impregnates wood pulp or rag paper with rubber. The trade name for its product, which is used for book covers, passport folders, gaskets, wall board, etc. is Lexide. Beaverite Products, Inc. does not make paper, but purchases materials and converts them into loose leaf binders, catalog covers, etc. Beaverite has two divisions in the area: at Glenfield, sheet plastic is used to make file dividers, sheet protectors and acetate envelopes; the Croghan plant is the die-casting division with its own tool shop, and it makes automobile gaskets and electrical insulation. In contrast to the two paper manufacturers, who employ mostly men, the workers at the Beaverite mills are for the most part women.

Though the French capital was to be at Beaver Falls, early attempts at settlement were not successful. The impetus which brought settlers came from Vincent Le Ray and his land agents. Between 1830 and 1850, 247 European families of 1,275 persons located in the towns of Croghan and New Bremen. These settlers, chiefly from eastern France, western Germany and Switzerland, selected land at from three to six dollars an acre. They paid one-fifth at the end of the first year, and the remainder after six years, plus interest. They settled in Dayanville (New Bremen), Prussian Settlement (Naumberg), French Settlement (Croghan) and Belfort.

Croghan, which got its name from Col. George Croghan, an Indian fighter under William Henry Harrison of Tippecanoe fame, is still the commercial center of the Beaver River valley, though it can look back on more prosperous days, when the big Rice tannery and two sawmills stood beside the river, and a dozen drinking places catered to the thirst of lumberjacks coming out of the woods for a spree. These woodsmen loved fine clothes. Before doing a round of the saloons, they would buy expensive suits, silk shirts and socks, and even silk underwear. Togged up in this finery, they would fight among themselves and return to camp with aching heads and ruined clothes.

Croghan lost a thriving industry in 1960, when the United Block Company plant burned and was not rebuilt. It still has a division of Beaverite and the Lehman-Zehr Lumber Company operating along the Beaver River, and in recent years the long-established firm of Campany Bros. and Nuspfliger has made "Croghan Bologna" famous throughout the North Country. This firm, which operates the Croghan Meat Market, has profited so much from "word of mouth" advertising that it produces 2,800 pounds of bologna each week.

Traces of Croghan's past are everywhere to be found. T. B. Basselin's mansion, with its porte-cochére, its sentinel lions, and its Greek statuary, is the home of Gerald Spencer, stock-broker son of Basselin's personal physician. Down the main street, five Basselins lie in splendid isolation in the family graveyard. A general store, founded by Edward M. Marilley, a French-Swiss immigrant, was burned and rebuilt and is now operated by Ralph Marilley, a son of its founder. Along the road to Belfort, descendants of Christian Zehr, a "Hook and Eye" Baptist who fought his way through the wilderness in 1832, are operating prosperous farms.

Croghan, like many villages in the North Country, has suffered severely from fire. On April 24, 1902, a conflagration wiped out St. Stephen's Church, a Franciscan monastery and convent, a parochial school, three stores, two hotels and seven houses. The church center was rebuilt under the leadership of Rev. Leo Heinrich, O. F. M. Croghan folks held Fr. Heinrich in the highest regard and when news came from Denver, Colorado years later that their beloved priest had been murdered by a religious fanatic, they named their new parochial school, built mainly through funds supplied by T. B. Basselin, Father Leo Memorial School.

On April 20, 1912, the village was practically wiped out by a raging holocaust which swept down both sides of the main street from the Colligan House to the Basselin mansion on one side and St. Stephen's Church on the other. Thirty-two buildings were destroyed and two small children lost their lives.

Croghan stands as a splendid example of religious toleration. The villagers are predominantly Roman Catholic, with St. Stephen's Church, Father Leo's School, a home for teaching nuns and a seminary where young men are trained as brothers in the Franciscan Order. The surrounding countryside is inhabited by Mennonites who are excellent farmers and who support three churches on the outskirts of the village. Though many of the early religious customs are observed, the younger generation of Mennonites use modern machinery and automobiles and send their children to the Beaver River Central School at Beaver Falls.

Naumberg, a sprawling village on the eastern side of the Black River near where the Beaver dumps its water into that stream, is characterized by large farms, most of them operated by descendants of the German immigrants who founded Prussian Settlement.

On the western bank of the river, the remains of Basselin's big sawmill are practically obliterated, but the village of Castorland, located on the railroad a stone's throw from the river, boasts a thriving industry. Back in 1906, Samuel and Urban Hirschey began the manufacture of incubators and cheese boxes on a small scale. Three years later, they formed the Climax Manufacturing Company and added paper flower boxes to their line. Climax makes no paper at Castorland, but gets board from the Carthage Papermakers, Inc. in West Carthage, which Climax purchased in 1935. Climax at Castorland employs 225 people and manufactures 500 types of boxes, which are colored, printed, cut and stripped, and shipped flat to customers, ready to fold and supplied with glue when necessary. In 1951, Climax added a new laminating and storage building and, in 1962, put up a building to take care of added business resulting from its purchase of the Brooklyn Folding Box Company. Climax, like many of the industries along the Black River, began as a family affair and has remained in that category, for Charles S. Hirschey, son of Urban Hirschey, is the president.

Denmark has changed little over the years. It never was a commercial center and today its background is agriculture. Several houses of native stone grace its main street and Freedom Wright's tavern, the birthplace of Jefferson and Lewis counties, has been converted into an attractive residence.

On the eastern shore of the Black River, directly opposite the point where the Deer River enters that stream, the Carthage Rod and Gun Club occupies the attractive, tree-laden shore settled as Sisterfield by Louis François de Saint Michel

before the close of the eighteenth century and later the entertainment park known and loved as Cold Spring Park.

Carthage and its "twin" village, West Carthage, offer a
sharp contrast to Lowville. The agricultural hinterland ends
abruptly at the Black River at the Long Falls, and industrial
development begins. The Long Falls with their water power
cried out for use in the early days, and it was on the islands in
the river that tanning, iron furnaces and allied industries
sprang up. By 1839, the villages boasted two blast furnaces,
one cupola furnace, two forges manufacturing 150 tons of
wrought iron annually, a nail factory, an oil mill and a flax
mill. With the coming of the Black River Canal, Carthage
became a shipping depot for iron, hides and lumber and
seemed destined to become the hub of industry in the North
Country, but the village encountered evil days. Tanning fell
by the wayside, lumber shipments declined, and the Carthage
Iron Company closed up because of a lowering of the price
of pig iron. The fire of 1884 seemed to seal the fate of the
twin villages.

Paper and Jim Outterson saved them. Carthage, forgetting
about lumber, iron and the fire, embarked on an industry
which still remains pre-eminent in the village. Paper-making
has survived two wars and several depressions, though it has
hit highs and lows over the years.

Three of the mills built just before the turn of the century
are no longer in operation. The Island Paper Company has
not operated since the first Roosevelt administration. Walter
Pratt of Boonville, who owned the mill at that time, was an
eccentric individualist who supplied the Black River valley
with enough anecdotes to fill a book. Pratt put up his back
when the Wage-Hour Act was passed. According to Carthaginians who knew him, Pratt announced that "no s. o. b.
in Washington was going to tell him what he would pay his
employes and the number of hours per week he could work
them." He got his men together, told them that he would
make no paper at the Island mill, but that they could stay

on as long as they wished at his expense. He kept the staff at work, "puttering" in the old mill. As wages rose and other jobs opened up, the men left, one by one. The mill stood in lonely isolation for thirty years, gathering weeds and slowly crumbling to pieces. After Pratt's death in 1962, in order to settle his estate—he left no will—the machinery was sold and one of the roofs has caved in.

The Carthage Tissue Paper Mills, located across from the railroad station, was rescued by the National Paper Products Company in 1917, and it was here that the first paper towels in the eastern part of the United States were manufactured. This mill is now used as a storage plant by the Crown Zellerbach Corporation.

The Champion Paper Company, on the West Carthage side of the river, became a division of the St. Regis Paper Company and was operated by that firm for a number of years, but it was closed two years ago, though it evidently is being kept up, for smoke curls from its tall stack.

The Carthage Pulp and Paper Company almost suffered a similar fate. In 1923, the old Outterson sulphite mill connected with the plant went up in flames. The mill closed down for some years and then was operated on a limited basis. In 1935, Urban Hirschey of the Climax Manufacturing Company of Castorland saw possibilities in the mill and he needed board to use at his growing plant in Castorland. Though the old pulp and paper mill was terribly rundown, Hirschey renovated it, bought the best water wheel available, and Climax, as the Carthage Papermakers, Inc., has been making board out of waste paper and other materials at West Carthage for 28 years.

Whereas the paper-making industry in Carthage had been started through use of local capital and the efforts of local men, the industry received an unexpected shot in the arm when Crown Zellerbach, a Pacific Coast firm, purchased the Carthage Tissue Paper Company in 1917. The Carthage Division of Crown Zellerbach now occupies what was once the West End Pulp and Casket Company and later the West End Paper Company, which the company took over in 1927.

Crown Zellerbach, since that time, has developed into the "bread and butter" industry of Carthage. It employs over 350 workers and has an annual payroll of $1,250,000. Its Carthage Division specializes in high quality toweling and facial tissues. It does not rely on local timber lands for pulp, but ships huge quantities of long-fiber pulp from mills located on the Pacific Coast. In providing steady employment to so many workers, it has given a boost to commercial life in Carthage and to farmers in the hinterland.

Good mechanics have remained in Carthage. The manufacture and installation of machinery for pulp and paper mills, started by Alexander Wendler before 1900, is still carried on by the Carthage Machine Company. Present production reflects changes in the times. Pumps, wet-machines and grinders are no longer manufactured by the Carthage Machine Company, which specializes in splitters and chippers. The company makes about a dozen large chippers each year for such firms as the Gould Paper Company and the St. Regis Paper Company. Small chippers are produced in larger quantities for use by small sawmills. The firm employs 85, mostly men.

The great wave of newsprint manufacture along the Black River from Carthage to Dexter has long since passed. Whereas a dozen mills were turning out newsprint as fast as their machines could make it forty years ago, no mill on the river is manufacturing newsprint today. Several factors have caused the change: spruce timber became increasingly scarce; labor troubles interfered with operation about the time of the First World War; tariff on Canadian newsprint was removed in the Twenties. Manufacturers of newsprint along the Black River could not compete with Canadian newsprint, which had at its disposal an ample supply of spruce, bigger and faster machines and encountered no labor troubles. As a result, newsprint mills along the river have disappeared. The only survivor is the St. Regis Paper Company, which has adjusted itself to other methods of manufacture.

When the St. Regis Paper Company was re-organized in 1916, its directors, with commendable foresight, purchased huge acreage in timber lands, both in the Adirondacks and in Canada. This foresight has paid off, for St. Regis is still able to manufacture pulp and paper at Deferiet in large quantities at a time when its competitors along the Black River have disappeared. Wood is brought to Deferiet from surrounding timber lands, but chiefly from Canada, where it is transported over a company railroad to the St. Lawrence River, shipped via the Seaway to Waddington, and carried by train to Deferiet. What the directors in 1916 could not have foreseen was the tremendous development of the St. Regis Paper Company, which now operates innumerable plants throughout the United States and in several foreign countries. The large mill at Deferiet has been reduced to the status of a division of the company, but its employes, a few of whom have been with St. Regis almost from the start, are proud of being the "charter members" of the firm.

The Deferiet Division at present is operating a six-machine mill, manufacturing ground wood printing papers and catalog book covers. The finished product is shipped to converters, both in rolls and in sheets. The Herrings Division specializes in Kraft papers. The Taggart mills at Great Bend and Felts Mills, once part of the St. Regis development, are mere ruins against the banks of the river.

The St. Regis Paper Company employs 925 people at its divisions in Deferiet and Herrings. Deferiet, conceived as a company village, no longer occupies that position. The village is incorporated and the company houses were sold to individual owners about eleven years ago.

The villages of Great Bend, Felts Mills and Black River, pioneers in lumbering and in pulp and paper manufacture, have lost their industries and residents depend upon St. Regis and Watertown for employment. A feature of Great Bend is the Woolworth Memorial Methodist Church, an edifice in the New England style, built for the people of the village by F. W. Woolworth, the five-and-dime tycoon, who was brought up in Great Bend.

The river between Deferiet and Watertown, though devoid of manufacturing plants, is being used by several big hydroelectric developments. The Niagara Mohawk Power Corporation produces electricity at Black River and at Diamond Island, while the Watertown municipal plant is located at Delano Island.

Watertown, the only city in the Black River valley, still reigns supreme as the capital of the North Country, though it has been deprived of some of the factors which contributed to its growth. Paper-making, once a leading industry, has practically disappeared, as has the making of flour. The decline of passenger service on the railroads has resulted in the sale of the Watertown station to the city and its removal along with considerable trackage. Of the many hotels which once catered to Watertown visitors, only the Woodruff House, now the Hotel Woodruff, with 250 rooms, maintains the status of a first-class establishment, though bright new motels may be found within the city limits. The business center of the city has remained unchanged for years, though the new plant of the *Watertown Daily Times* and the construction this year of a new home for the now Marine Midland Trust Company give indications that Watertown is on the move. Two promising projects, an urban renewal development in the heart of the city and the formation of Jefferson Community College, have encountered obstacles which may take considerable tact to hurdle.

Watertown, from the days of Henry Coffeen, has relied on industry for its livelihood. At the core of its success has been the excellent water power furnished by the Black River. Over the past century and a half, a steady stream of industry has flourished on both banks of the river and on Beebee's Island and Sewall's Island. This list is impressive—sawmills, gristmills, flouring mills, pulp and paper mills, sewing machine and carriage-making plants, portable steam engines, paper-making machinery, iron-working plants and vacuum brakes for locomotives. Industries have risen, flourished, declined and died as the demand for their product ceased or better facilities for producing it existed elsewhere.

As of 1963, but one important paper-making industry has survived in Watertown. Gone are the dreams of the Remingtons and the Taggarts and the International Paper Company. The sole representative of the paper industry in Watertown is the pioneer, Knowlton Brothers. This company, with an old mill, has been forced to adjust itself to changes within the industry and has done so remarkably well. Knowlton Brothers were never big operators like the Remingtons and the Taggarts. They had started on a shoestring and have adjusted their operations to the fluctuations in the demand. They never went into the production of newsprint in quantity, but have experimented with colored paper and other types as the necessity arose. At present, Knowlton Brothers can adapt themselves to almost any demand of a customer. They get pulp from Canada, the United States and Scandinavia, bleach for kraft from Sweden and Canada, high alpha sulphite from Washington and Florida, and cotton linter pulp from Tennessee and Virginia. In manufacturing specialty products, they use leather, kapok, glass, asbestos, ceramics, cork, manila rope, synthetic fibers such as nylon, dacron and dynal, and even import esparto grass from France. They make shotgun shell paper, filter papers for oil, air and fuels, saturating and impregnating papers, artificial leather, laminating paper for electrical insulation, gas mask filter papers, photograph wrapping and interlaying papers, radio and TV loud speaker cone paper, and a special paper for Western Union telefax machines. Though the exterior of the Knowlton Brothers mill betrays its age, the offices and factory rooms have been modernized, and the company operates a special test laboratory for experimentation.

The thriving industries which once flourished at Factory Square and on Sewall's Island have gone, with the exception of Bagley & Sewall, which began making paper-making machines way back in 1889. The firm operated under the long-established name until 1954, though it was owned by Abe Cooper from 1939 to 1954. In the latter year, it was purchased by the Black Clawson Company of Hamilton, Ohio, the world's leading manufacturer of machinery for the pulp and paper industry. Huge paper-making machines are made at the Watertown Division at the rate of seven or eight each year. These machines are a far cry from the fourdriniers which made paper in Watertown and vicinity fifty years ago. Whereas a 100-inch machine which could operate at a speed of 300 feet per minute was considered perfection at that time, Bagley & Sewall produced, in 1958, for the Great Lakes Paper Company of Fort William, Ontario, a 342-inch machine capable of operating at a speed of 2,000 feet per minute. The Paper Machine Division of the Black Clawson at Watertown manufactures fourdrinier and cylinder paper and board machines, structural board machines and auxiliary equipment. Seven or eight paper-making machines a year may seem small production until one is informed that these machines sell for from 1½ to five million dollars each, depending on the size. The Black Clawson Company, in addition to its main mill, operates a foundry and two large machine shops and uses familiar buildings, including the Excelsior Carriage Company mill and part of the Taggart Paper & Bag Company plant, for pattern storage and research laboratories. It employs 600 people.

Relics of Watertown's industrial past can be seen on all sides. Small, specialized industries occupy several buildings on Sewall's Island and at Factory Square. The H. H. Babcock Carriage Company, once the pride of Watertown, still has its name stamped prominently on its old building, now part of the Abe Cooper Watertown Corporation, an iron-salvage concern. The Harmon Machine Company was absorbed by

Bagley & Sewall and the J. B. Wise company mill, minus one story, is occupied by Wilbur's Discount City. The Taggart Paper & Bag Company, operated by the St. Regis Paper Company from 1944 to 1954, was purchased by Abe Cooper in the latter year and has reverted to its original name, though no paper is being made at the mill at present.

The water power of the Black River, which encouraged early pioneers to settle at Watertown and which contributed mightily to the city's development as a manufacturing center, is no longer the significant factor in today's industrial life. The uncontrolled river, with its floods in spring and its low water in summer, has forced mills to rely less and less on water wheels for operation and to depend upon electric power supplied by the Niagara-Mohawk Power Corporation, with plants at Black River, Diamond Island, Sewall's Island and Beebee's Island.

The New York Air Brake Company moved away from the river in 1910. Its sprawling plant near Pearl Street is now the Watertown Division of the company, which has its headquarters in New York City. Other plants are located in Aurora, Illinois; Providence, Rhode Island; Natick and Boston, Massachusetts; Kalamazoo, Michigan; Camden, New Jersey and Poole, Dorset, England. The Watertown Division, which employs 1286 workers, still makes air brakes for locomotives and railroad cars, but its Dynapower Section manufactures high-pressure hydrostatic transmission systems, piston type hydraulic pumps, motors and valves for special types of mobile equipment, fan and compressor drives and hydraulic servo systems. Its Stratopower Section serves the missile, space and aircraft industries with high-pressure hydraulic pumps, motors, valves, jet engine hydraulic starters and integrated component systems. Like Knowlton Brothers, Air Brake has been able to adjust itself to the changes in the times.

Watertown would like to attract more heavy industry and efforts are being made to do so, but its geographical location works to its disadvantage. Heavy industry likes to find raw materials near at hand and a ready nearby market for its product. Watertown can no longer supply raw materials, as it did during the boom years, when an ample spruce supply kept the paper mills in full operation and grain from nearby farms made the city an important flour-milling center. The North Country, with its sparse population, never absorbed the products of the industries along the river, but depended upon an outside market which was reached by railroad. The rapidly increasing cost of transportation, both by railroad and by truck, has added considerably to the cost of raw materials and to the price of finished products. There is also the factor of the long, hard North Country winters, which add to operating expenses through bills for heating plants and for snow removal.

Diversification of industry may be Watertown's hope for the future. Manufacturing is still being carried on throughout the city. Factory Square and Sewall's Island house small industries and about 40 plants in the city are making everything from straw hats, clothing and thermometers to snow plows and garbage trucks. Watertown, boasting an ample supply of skilled labor and excellent labor relations, should be able to adapt itself to changing conditions in the industrial world.

Watertown, with a population of under 34,000, serves as the hub of governmental, commercial and cultural life for Jefferson County. It is true today that "all roads lead to Watertown," for the highways, like the railroads, converge at the capital of the North Country. The city also maintains a municipal airport on the road to Sackets Harbor. The Jefferson County Courthouse, built during the Civil War, plus other buildings, including the Roswell P. Flower mansion, house the various governmental agencies. Watertown has two commercial banks: The Watertown National Bank is a descendant of the Jefferson County Bank; The Northern New York Trust Company has become affiliated with the Marine Midland Trust Company. There are three savings banks in the city; the Jefferson County Savings Bank, the Watertown

Savings Bank and the Savings and Loan Association of Watertown. The Agricultural Insurance Company occupies an imposing building on Washington Street. The city is well-equipped with stores which attract customers from a far-flung area. On the cultural side, the city not only possesses excellent elementary and secondary schools, but is at present trying to get the Jefferson Community College off the ground. The Little Theatre of Watertown presents three plays each year; the Watertown Community Concert Association sponsors four concerts a season; the Watertown Artists Guild holds one annual indoor exhibit and a sidewalk show; the North Country Bird Club finds that its five Audubon lectures draw large and appreciative audiences.

Watertown, during the nineteenth century, produced many men who rose to leadership in the city and the State. They never forgot the North Country city to which they owed their start, and Watertown has been the beneficiary of countless gifts from these self-made men and their families. Washington Street, the most attractive thoroughfare in the North Country, offers testimony to their generosity. The Y.M.C.A. Building was the gift of John A. Sherman, a butter and cheese merchant from Rutland who later lived in Watertown. The Jefferson County Historical Society was willed its present home by the widow of E. L. Paddock of the mercantile family of that name. The Flower Memorial Library, the most attractive building in the city and one of the finest libraries in the State, was the gift of Mrs. Emma Flower Taylor, daughter of Roswell P. Flower, the only North Country man to serve as Governor of New York. The Henry Keep Home has stood since 1883 as a memorial to the friendless orphan whose "rags to riches" career could have come right out of a Horatio Alger paperback. Keep, after undergoing poverty and hardship, rose to the presidency of the New York Central Railroad. The home, the gift of Mrs. Keep, who was a daughter of Norris W. Woodruff of hotel fame, is still in operation after 80 years.

These gifts were made without undo fanfare, but the donors were usually known at the time. This was not so with Thompson Park, located on the heights overlooking the city and reached by Thompson Boulevard, which leads off from Washington Street. Back in 1900, a real-estate man, Henry D. Goodale, purchased 700 acres on Pinnacle Hill and a noted architect, John C. Olmstead, began to landscape the area. The Olmsteads believed in the theory that "nature abhors a straight line," so winding drives were laid out to the hill. City Park, with its zoo, picnic grounds and play areas, soon supplanted Glen Park as the recreational ground for Watertown folks. In 1924, John C. Thompson, president of the New York Air Brake Company, died, and the public was informed that the beautiful park on Pinnacle Hill had been his gift to the city. In grateful appreciation, the people renamed the area Thompson Park.

No history of the Black River valley would be complete without mention of the *Watertown Daily Times*. The *Times* was but one of several newspapers in the city when Beman Brockway assumed responsibility for its publication in 1873. Brockway, who had edited several country newspapers and had been at one time a reporter with Horace Greeley's *New York Tribune*, brought along two sons, Jefferson W. and Henry A., both of whom had been acquainted with the smell of printers' ink since childhood. The firm name became B. Brockway & Sons. After the father's death in 1892, the name was changed to the Brockway Sons Company. Jefferson had progressive ideas. Though the *Times* was staggering financially when his father took it over, he insisted that putting money into better presses would eventually help the newspaper. He won out over considerable opposition, and the *Times* gradually worked into a pre-eminent position in the city. By 1904, the *Times* had increased its circulation to 5,000, whereas the daily paper had reached but 700 when the Brockways took over. The Brockways had died, but Henry's widow still maintained an active interest in the newspaper.

The man who was to make the *Times* the great newspaper of today came over from Governeur in 1904 to serve as a reporter. Harold B. Johnson understood the North Country. He was close to the lives of the people and was always conscious of their way of life. Year by year, he gradually assumed leadership of the *Times* until he eventually became the editor and publisher. He conducted a running battle with the *Watertown Standard* until 1929, when that paper "threw in the towel" and sold out to Johnson, "lock, stock and barrel." Harold Johnson was not only a superb newspaper man, but he was vitally interested in all projects which might improve conditions in the North Country. His friendship with Edward John Noble, which had started during their boyhood years in Governeur, made him an important figure in the Noble Foundation, which has contributed enormous sums of money to educational institutions and hospitals in the North Country. His untimely death in 1949 deprived the Black River valley of a leader and a friend.

John B. Johnson succeeded his father as editor and publisher. Though the young man had a big pair of shoes to fill, he has succeeded in doing so. The newspaper has increased its circulation to 45,000 and the *Times*, during the past year, has moved its entire facilities to a modern building on Washington Street. The *Times* has never been a sensational sheet. It believes in recording the news accurately and impartially. Although its coverage of national and international news is excellent, the Johnsons have never forgotten that their chief concern is to cover happenings in the North Country. The *Times* is probably the best-organized newspaper in the State; a reader does not have to thumb through a whole issue to find what he wishes to read. Though the *Times* contains much advertising, it is not placed where it will unduly intrude on the reader. An interesting innovation is that of starting regional feature articles on the last page of the paper, indicating that the *Times* senses that this position is secondary only to the first page, which features national and international news.

Editorial stands are boldly taken, and much space is devoted to comments and rebuttals from letter-writers throughout the North Country. John Johnson evidently feels, as his father did before him, that the *Times* is the Voice of the North Country, an open forum where news and views can be exchanged. And he is also involved in movements for progress in the area. If you don't think so, try to catch up with him.

Glen Park was once the heart of an industrial and recreational development. Today, Jim Wood's Falls flow freely toward the lake, for the industries which once flourished at the spot have long disappeared. Ruins against the banks of the Black River indicate mutely where the two Remington mills and the Ontario Paper Company once stood. These mills, purchased from the Remingtons in 1899, were operated for over twenty years by the International Paper Company which, faced by the combined forces of inadequate pulp supply, labor troubles and obsolete machinery, moved out and had the stone mills torn down.

Crumbling piers mark the site of the iron bridge which the Remingtons built across the river to reach their amusement ground on the south shore—the original Glen Park. Between 1890 and 1904, Glen Park, served by the Watertown and Brownville Electric Railroad, was the gathering place for thousands of pleasure-seekers from the Black River valley. Open-air cars equipped with brightly colored awnings made the trip on the electric railroad a must for all lovers of picnics. A natural amphitheater provided comfortable viewing points for spectators who thronged to Glen Park to see Watertown's famous professional football team, the Red and Black, overcome all rivals with ridiculous ease. A large pavilion attracted thousands to stage plays and to lectures by eminent people. The Watertown City Band gave concerts at the bandstand. Balloons ascended to the cheers of folks on the ground and tight-rope walkers risked their necks by performing feats over Jim Wood's Falls. The ancient caves, known to early settlers and mentioned by Dr. Hough, were opened up. Staircases with railings, and strings of electric lights guided sightseers on tours of the underground caverns. And, more than anything else, Glen Park was a picnic ground, with tables set under the tall trees where families could get together for meals under ideal conditions and Sunday School groups could enjoy days of pleasure. Glen Park was abandoned in 1904 and the electric railroad to Dexter in 1937. The amusement ground on the south side of the Black River has reverted to farm land.

Brownville also entered the amusement field toward the close of the nineteenth century. A little steamer named the "Grape Island Belle" took picnic parties down the scenic gorge to Grape Island near Dexter, where Henry Livermore held forth at the Grape Island Hotel. Livermore's venture was merely a passing fancy. The hotel is gone and the island is overgrown with brush.

Brownville, a small village with attractive homes and stores, basks in the shadow of its Quaker founder, whose home still stands and whose memory is preserved by signs at the entrances to the village and by an imposing school which is appropriately named the General Brown High School.

Two of Brownville's three factories are still in operation. The Brownville Paper Company, located on the site of the village's first cotton and woolen mill, has for years been the only manufacturer of fine paper along the river. Its product is known commercially as "Seafoam Bond." Across the bridge, on the south side of the river, the Brownville Board Company, now an affiliate of the J. P. Lewis Company of Beaver Falls, manufactures soap and cereal boxes and spacers for filing systems. The Harmon Paper Company, built by Jim Outterson, has been abandoned for years and is merely an imposing ruin featuring decaying stone walls and a tall smokestack.

Dexter, at the mouth of the Black River, offers tangible evidence of the rise, decline and fall of the paper-making industry. Twenty years ago, three large mills were in full operation at Dexter. Today, two are complete ruins and the third has been closed down. The St. Lawrence Paper Company mill, later operated as the Warren Parchment Company, was taken over by the Ron-Noc-O Paper Corporation in 1931. Two years later, it went back to the Warrens, who sold it to Robert E. Read, Inc. This company remodelled the mill, installed machinery which occupied the full three-and-a-half stories, and manufactured specialized paper products from wood pulp until 1942, when it filed a petition of bankruptcy. The Water Falls Paper Mills, a Maine concern, acquired title in 1946 and then sold out to the Dexter Sulphite Pulp & Paper Co. The career of the old mill, known affectionately in Dexter as "The Beanery," came to a close.

The Frontenac Paper Company mill, built on the site of the first sawmill on Fish Island, was taken over by the Dexter Sulphite Co. and completely remodelled in 1901. The Sulphite Co. operated it until 1947, when it again became the Frontenac Paper Company, under the ownership of I. Lawrence LeSavoy of New York. The mill closed in 1949 and in the following year was destroyed in a $100,000 fire.

The Dexter Sulphite Pulp & Paper Company, which moved into the old woolen mill in 1889, carried on under the management of Dr. James E. and Dr. Clarence W. Campbell until 1920, when it was purchased by William Randolph Hearst. The mill ran into financial difficulties in 1942 and was sold to K. C. Irving of St. John, New Brunswick. During World War II, the mill ran at full blast, but it again encountered evil days and was closed in 1953. As of 1963, it is owned by Abe Cooper of Watertown.

Industry at Dexter is confined to two small hydro-electric plants owned by Raymond B. Frank and operated as the Dexter Hydro-Electric Corp. These plants, like that of Raymond Bailey at Port Leyden, sell their product to the Niagara-Mohawk Power Corporation.

The ruins at Dexter are picturesque. Fishing is still good near the dam at Fish Island. The village of Dexter, inhabited by people who find employment in Watertown and other places, keeps up an air of respectability, though its citizens realize that industry may never visit the village again.

Sackets Harbor cannot bemoan a loss of industry, but it too suffered a severe blow with the closing of Madison Barracks in 1945. The military character of the village persists only in the innumerable State markers which proclaim the deeds of the past. The site of the Battle of Sackets Harbor, located along Lake Ontario, is well kept up and is the goal of many historically-minded visitors each summer. The Pickering Museum and several attractive old buildings, including the Union Hotel and the mansion built by Elisha Camp of "Camp's Ditch" fame, remind the village of its illustrious past. Business life at the Harbor is at a low ebb and the mercantile section has not kept pace with the times. And, rankling in the minds of the residents is the fact that Madison Barracks, once the pride of the village, have been allowed to fall into a deplorable condition. Caved-in roofs, broken windows, traces of fires and boarded-up buildings make Madison Barracks an eye-sore overlooking Lake Ontario. Though a few of the buildings have been restored and are used as tenements, the overall appearance of Madison Barracks is so bedraggled that one ex-soldier who served there remarked sadly, "I simply can't go back and look at the place."

Dexter, long devoted to paper-making, and Sackets Harbor, once a proud military post village, are showing signs that they may adjust themselves to a new way of life. Black River Bay, an attractive inlet of Lake Ontario, offers splendid possibilities for future development. The bay is land-locked and free from the ill winds which often harass the lake. Attractive cottages are springing up along the shores and a big marina is under construction at Navy Point at the Harbor, where Henry Eckford turned out ships for the United States Navy during the War of 1812 and where the ill-fated "New Orleans" and its shiphouse attracted sentimental visitors for many years.

It appears obvious that the Black River valley must adjust its sights to the future. More heavy industry probably will not locate there, and it may be difficult to hold the ones which remain. Small, specialized industry may be the answer for Carthage, Lowville and Watertown, but small villages must rely more and more upon their agricultural resources and make a determined effort to attract tourists to the North Country.

Noadiah Hubbard, the first settler in Jefferson County, chose agriculture over industry. His village, Champion, has not changed much over the years. It is still a small community located in the midst of rolling farms. The Hubbard touch is on the village today: the stone houses which Noadiah built stand on the main street; gravestones sprinkled throughout the cemetery record the names of many Hubbards who have lived and died in the village; there are direct descendants of the founder tilling the land in Champion.

Back from the river, from above Lowville down through Champion, Rutland and Adams to Lake Ontario, the rolling country is a patchwork of fertile fields under cultivation. For the most part, the houses, barns and other farm buildings indicate, by the manner in which they are kept up, that farming is a prosperous business. True, farmers are often perplexed by governmental regulations and irritated by fluctuations in the price of milk; but, over the years, they have developed agriculture until it is the backbone of the Black River valley. With the decline of industry along the river, farming should become increasingly important in stabilizing the economy.

A more recent development which should prove a boon to the Black River valley is tourism. The river and its tributaries have many attractions to offer vacationists. The upper stretches of the Black, Moose and Beaver rivers flow through the Adirondack forest. Old Forge, on the middle branch of the Moose at the outlet of the Fulton Chain of lakes, has long been a favorite resort for tourists. The Adirondack League Club, though offering benefits to a selective few, uses a vast primitive vacation land on the south branch of the same river.

North, South and Honnedaga lakes, at and near the source of the Black River, have become camping paradises for thousands of nature lovers, fishermen and hunters. Kayuta Lake (Forestport Reservoir) gives much enjoyment to campers. Stillwater Reservoir on the Beaver also caters to vacationists. Campers are good for the economy of these areas, for they usually trade at stores in nearby villages.

The mouth of the Black River has even greater possibilities, for it lies adjacent to the Thousand Islands, an area which has been popular since 1872, when President Ulysses S. Grant paid a visit to the North Country and by that gesture lent prestige to the struggling young hotels. People of wealth blazed a trail to the Columbian, the Frontenac, the Grand View and other luxury hotels which were built in the following years. The Folger fleet of steamers connected with trains at Cape Vincent and Clayton and made eight stops between those villages and Alexandria Bay.

The Crosman at Alexandria Bay became symbolic of the spirit of the Gay Nineties. John A. Haddock wrote: "At night the Crosman, in-doors and out, presents a scene of brilliancy. Rows of colored lights illumine the verandas and shine from its many towers, shedding a wealth of color upon the water. The drawing-rooms are filled with guests engaged in social pastimes, and all about the place there is light and life and gayety. The arrival of the steamers at evening is celebrated by a display of fireworks in front of the hotel and on the neighboring islands, making a picture indescribably beautiful."

Wealthy people came to spend weeks at the Crosman and other hotels, and expensive mansions, including Boldt's Castle, were constructed on the islands. The Thousand Islands became the jewel of the North Country.

The old order showed signs of change as early as 1874, when a group of prominent Methodists, led by Rev. J. F. Dayan, purchased 1,000 acres on Wells (Wellesley) Island

and started what is known as Thousand Island Park. Land for cottages was sold in small plots at low prices, and the response was so enthusiastic that the sales on the first day reached $22,000.

Thousand Island Park was designed for men of little wealth, and since the time of its inception the vast vacationland along Black River Bay, the St. Lawrence River and on the Thousand Islands has been opened up for the enjoyment of the common man.

The era of the luxury hotel has passed. The Columbian and other massive structures fell victim to fire, and the imposing Crosman was torn down in 1962.

The age of the automobile has made people more restless. They do not wish to spend entire vacations at one spot. As a result, numerous motels have sprung up in the villages and along the highways where tourists can spend nights comfortably before going on with their travels.

Wealthy people still come to spend summers in their mansions, but the bulk of traffic through the North Country consists of folks with lesser means. To cater to this class of tourist, the State has, within recent years, built a dozen or more camping sites from Henderson Harbor to Alexandria Bay. For a small fee, families can rent a site, put up a tent, and enjoy excellent camping, boating, fishing and swimming facilities.

Watertown and other North Country communities are becoming increasingly conscious of the value of catering to the thousands of vacationists who visit them each summer. The Greater Watertown Chamber of Commerce, though trying desperately to bring more industry to the area, recently issued a pamphlet which proclaims Watertown as the "Gateway to the Thousand Islands and Canada."

XX
SPRING, 1963

THE BLACK RIVER staged a spectacular performance during the first week of April, 1963. A warm spell and a pouring rain loosened the snowbanks on Tug Hill. The Sugar River and the Deer River became raging torrents, pouring tons of turbulent water into the Black River, which was also on the rise. The Black River at Lyons Falls, swollen by the contribution of the Sugar River and to some extent by that of the Moose, rose to such a height that the Gould Paper Company had to halt operations for the first time in 29 years. The Deer River at Copenhagen overflowed its banks, flooded many cellars in the village, and contaminated the water supply. "Lake Lewis" covered the farm lands from above Glenfield to Carthage. Communications between villages on opposite shores of the Black River were broken for over a week, and remnants of the lake were visible until mid-May.

Engineers constructing a new Beach's Bridge had spent the previous autumn creating a dike with culverts to contain the expected surge of the Black River. The rushing stream ignored these obstacles; it merely coursed on in its turbulent manner and took the dike with it. Folks wishing to go from Lowville to Watson could not get within a quarter of a mile of Beach's Bridge. At the height of the flood, a store caught fire in Watson. The Lowville Fire Department, in order to reach the scene of the conflagration, had to travel twenty miles by way of the Naumberg-Castorland Bridge. Needless to say, the store was destroyed.

Dexter, at the mouth of the Black River, felt the full impact of the surging water. The Long Bridge, which had withstood many floods, shook and heaved so badly that it had to be blocked off. Trucks drew gravel from Watertown during a day and a night so that workers could build a temporary dike along William Street. The village lighting system failed, and workers labored under flood lights supplied by the Glen Park Fire Department. Despite herculean efforts by the firemen and workers, the river spilled over into the village and flooded cellars.

A sudden drop in temperature prevented what might have been the most serious flood along the Black River in many years. People kept their fingers crossed, waiting for the snow in the Adirondacks to melt and send the Moose River into its annual flood. Luckily, the ground had not been frozen when the first heavy snowfall had come in the preceding November, so much of the snow was absorbed by the forest instead of running off in torrents. The Moose, though it cascaded spectacularly from Lyonsdale to Lyons Falls, did not reach its highest flood stage, and the people of the Black River valley breathed a collective sigh of relief.

The Black River and its tributaries are beautiful streams. The people love them and are grateful for the contributions they have made to the industrial development of the valley, but they feel that something must be done to prevent the annual floodings which cause damage, inconvenience and harassment to villages along their courses.

Despite the irritations and inconveniences caused by the irresponsible rivers, folks in the Black River valley probably are more appreciative of spring than any similar group in the United States. Before the disappearance of the last snowbank, farmers are at work, plowing their fields and fertilizing them. Pungent smoke curls softly from sugar bushes standing aloof from the highways. Cows tread gingerly through the still-wet fields in search of the first blades of grass. Lawn-mowers hum in the villages and houses begin to show signs of new paint. Industry perks up in anticipation of spring orders. Along the streams, fishermen try to lure the evasive trout and, at the mouth of the river, villagers prepare for the anticipated influx of tourists.

"For, lo, the winter is past," seems to rise to the lips of some of the finest people in the whole world.

Bibliographical Notes

The first and ablest historian of the North Country was Dr. Franklin B. Hough of Lowville. Two of his histories, *A History of Jefferson County* (Albany, 1854) and *A History of Lewis County* (Albany, 1860), constitute basic works upon which all later historians have relied heavily for information on the Black River region. *The Documentary History of New York* (Albany, 1850) edited by E. B. O'Callaghan, M. D., contains early maps and documents relating to Samuel de Champlain and the Jesuits. *Lake Ontario*, by Arthur Pound (Indianapolis-New York, 1945) gives an authoritative account of the history near the mouth of the Black River from 1615 to 1783. Volume I of *The North Country*, by Harry F. Landon (Indianapolis, 1932) covers these years in more detail than Pound's book, particularly in relation to events occurring in and affecting the Black River area.

Émigrés in the Wilderness, by Dr. T. Wood Clarke (New York, 1941) deals interestingly, but not always accurately, with the settlements of James Le Ray de Chaumont and other French landlords. *North of the Mohawk*, by Hilda Doyle Merriam (Chicago, 1950) covers much of the same material, but not as thoroughly as the Clarke book.

A History of Lewis County, by Dr. Franklin B. Hough (Syracuse, 1883) amplifies some of the material in Dr. Hough's early history and carries events down to 1883. *A History of Jefferson County*, by John A. Haddock (Philadelphia, 1894) uses much of the Hough material. Though badly organized, it contains a wealth of information regarding industrial life along the Black River, anecdotes about the North Country, and countless biographies of prominent citizens, many of whom Haddock knew personally.

Three books by Thomas C. O'Donnell, *Snubbing Posts* (Boonville, 1949), *Birth of a River* (Boonville, 1952), and *The River Rolls on* (Prospect, 1959) are informal histories of the Black River Canal and the Black River from North Lake to Carthage. They contain invaluable information about lumbering and boating activities along the canal and the river. A series of articles by Ralph N. and Lewis S. Van Arnam, *The Era of Navigation on the Black River* (*North Country Life*, Saranac, 1949), present an excellent and authoritative picture of that phase of Black River history.

A History of the Adirondacks, by Alfred L. Donaldson (New York, 1921) contains in Volume I a careful account of the Macomb Purchase and in Volume II some excellent observations on lumbering, forest control and legislation involving the establishment of the Forest Preserve. *Adirondack Country*, by William Chapman White (New York and Boston, 1954) comments shrewdly on the same subjects.

Power and Storage Possibilities of the Black River, a report of the Division of Waters of the State of New York Conservation Commission (Albany, 1919), gives a detailed account of surveys made and descriptions of possible sites for reservoirs. *Water for New York*, by Roscoe C. Martin (Syracuse, 1960) is probably the most comprehensive study of the struggle between the conservationists and the flood control groups over the proposed building of a dam at Panther Mountain.

From Saints to Red Legs, by Gordon G. Heiner (Watertown, undated) carries the history of Madison Barracks from the years of their construction to 1937. *The Rise and Fall of the Patriot Hunters*, by Oscar A. Kinchen (New York, 1956) is a good account of the Patriot War.

The following localized histories have been helpful in pinpointing events: *A Brief Historical Sketch of Carthage, New York*, by William D. Welsh, based on a manuscript by Floyd J. Rich (Carthage, 1955) *History of Dexter, New York*, compiled by Marion H. Evans (1955) *Welcome to Camp Drum* (undated) *Centennial History of the Village of Lowville, N. Y.*, Historical Committee, Jos. W. Singer, Chairman (1954) *History of Lyons Falls*, by Clarence L. Fisher (1914) *Tales from Little Lewis*, by Hazel C. Drew (1961) and *150 Years of Watertown*, by Harry F. Landon (Watertown, 1950), this last book being a fascinating account of Watertown from the time of settlement until 1950.

Information has been gleaned from articles in the following magazines: *The Ad-i-ron-dac*, published by the Adirondack Mountain Club, *North Country Life* (Saranac) and *The Northeastern Logger* (Old Forge). The last-named magazine contains, in its May, 1960 issue, A. B. Recknagel's excellent article telling how Albrecht Pagenstecher introduced Voelter grinders into the United States; also a comprehensive account of the achievements of John E. Johnston.

And, finally, the files of the *Watertown Daily Times* have been the source of considerable information. Of particular value have been a series of articles on paper-making by Howard W. Palmer in Scrapbook No. 74 and two articles by David F. Lane (Nov. 15 and 16, 1960) on hydro-electric development in Watertown.